About This Book

Why is this topic important?

Today's increasingly mobile, decentralized workforce presents challenges to im-proving job performance that didn't exist just a few years ago. As the Baby Boom generation begins to retire, corporations must find new ways to train a younger generation of workers who are often dispersed geographically and have limited time for training.

For such workers, who have grown up using advanced technologies, the method of distributing multimedia files over the Internet called *podcasting* offers an excellent option. Podcasting makes it possible to address many of the geographic, logistical, and generational issues that today's training professionals face. Podcasts, which can be downloaded to mobile devices such as iPods or to personal computers, do not confine their users to a geographic location or a scheduled time, so they are excellent tools for delivering information and training on demand. The material can be updated every time the device is connected to the Internet. Perhaps most attractive is the fact that there is virtually no learning curve required for the millions of employees who already use such devices. Fourteen million iPods were sold in the fourth quarter of 2005 alone and forty-two million have been sold since the first quarter of 2004. In 2006, 40 percent of cars sold in the United States had iPod integration, and airplanes now have iPod integration too.

What can you achieve with this book?

This book can help you revolutionize the way you deliver training. It provides an approach to designing and developing podcasts that improve employees' productivity by providing them with easy-to-access, up-to-date information. This book will help you to decide if podcasting is the right solution for the business problem your organization is facing, and then help you make the right decisions in selecting the software and hardware that you will use to create your podcasts. It will introduce you to the legal issues surrounding podcast development, expose you to an approach to developing podcasts that will ensure that your podcasts make a positive business impact, and finally it will teach you how to plan, record, edit, and publish a training podcast.

How is this book organized?

This book has two parts. Part One explores the business case for podcasting, looks at podcasting as a training option, introduces the podcasting development process, provides an overview of the hardware and software you will need, and includes a discussion of legal issues related to podcasting. Part Two provides a step-by-step approach for developing and distributing podcasts.

About Pfeiffer

Pfeiffer serves the professional development and hands-on resource needs of training and human resource practitioners and gives them products to do their jobs better. We deliver proven ideas and solutions from experts in HR development and HR management, and we offer effective and customizable tools to improve workplace performance. From novice to seasoned professional, Pfeiffer is the source you can trust to make yourself and your organization more successful.

Essential Knowledge Pfeiffer produces insightful, practical, and comprehensive materials on topics that matter the most to training and HR professionals. Our Essential Knowledge resources translate the expertise of seasoned professionals into practical, how-to guidance on critical workplace issues and problems. These resources are supported by case studies, worksheets, and job aids and are frequently supplemented with CD-ROMs, websites, and other means of making the content easier to read, understand, and use.

Essential Tools Pfeiffer's Essential Tools resources save time and expense by offering proven, ready-to-use materials—including exercises, activities, games, instruments, and assessments—for use during a training or team-learning event. These resources are frequently offered in looseleaf or CD-ROM format to facilitate copying and customization of the material.

Pfeiffer also recognizes the remarkable power of new technologies in expanding the reach and effectiveness of training. While e-hype has often created whizbang solutions in search of a problem, we are dedicated to bringing convenience and enhancements to proven training solutions. All our e-tools comply with rigorous functionality standards. The most appropriate technology wrapped around essential content yields the perfect solution for today's on-the-go trainers and human resource professionals.

Essential resources for training and HR professionals

In memory of my mother, Ruby Cayne,
the woman who shaped my character
and the character of so many others.

Pfeiffer™

Podcasting 101 for Training and Development

Kaliym A. Islam

John Wiley & Sons, Inc.

Published by Pfeiffer
An Imprint of Wiley
989 Market Street, San Francisco, CA 94103-1741

www.pfeiffer.com

Wiley Bicentennial logo: Richard J. Pacificio

For additional copies/bulk purchases of this book in the U.S. please contact 800-274-4434.

Pfeiffer books and products are available through most bookstores. To contact Pfeiffer directly call our Customer Care Department within the U.S. at 800-274-4434, outside the U.S. at 317-572-3985, fax 317-572-4002, or visit www.pfeiffer.com.

Pfeiffer also publishes its books in a variety of electronic formats. Some content that appears in print may not be available in electronic books.

Library of Congress Cataloging-in-Publication Data

Islam, Kaliym A.
    Podcasting 101 for training and development : challenges, opportunities, and solutions / Kaliym A. Islam.
        p. cm.
    Includes index.
    ISBN 978-0-7879-8849-4 (pbk.)
    1. Employees–Training of–Computer-assisted instruction. 2. Podcasting. 3. Employees–Training of–Computer network resources. 4. Web-based instruction. 5. Educational technology. I. Title. II. Title: Podcasting one zero one for training and development. III. Title: Podcasting one zero and one for training and development.
HF5549.5.T7I783 2007
658.3'124028567875–dc22

                                                                                    2007013436

Acquiring Editor: Matthew Davis   Production Editor: Michael Kay
Marketing Manager: Jeanenne Ray   Editorial Assistant: Julie Rodriguez
Director of Development: Kathleen Dolan Davies Editor: Hilary Powers
Editorial Assistant: Julie Rodriguez   Manufacturing Supervisor: Becky Morgan

Printed in the United States of America

Printing   10 9 8 7 6 5 4 3 2 1

Contents

List of Tables, Figures, and Exhibits

Tables

Figures

Exhibits

Foreword

It's a no-brainer. In order to improve an
organization's performance, the performance of the
workers who make up that organization must first be
improved. Today, organizations face challenges that
did not exist just a few years ago . . . new workers are
also far more technologically savvy than their
parents. Having grown up with computers, cell
phones, personal electronic devices, mobile audio
players, and the Internet, the children of the Baby
Boomers expect instant communication.

—*Kaliym A. Islam*

These statements say it all. In fact, the Gartner group indicates that within a year, 80 percent of all enterprises will have at least 50 percent of their knowledge workers engaged in some form of telecommuting or other nomadic work. They go so far as to suggest that workplace transformation is a critical management imperative for the connected economy as a key to attract, retain, and enable talented employees, and to reallocate financial resources between physical and digital infrastructure.

For years I have watched as Kaliym Islam has promoted the application of business processes, innovations, techniques, and technologies to training programs. His landmark book, *Developing and Measuring Training the Six Sigma Way,* presented the training industry with an alternative to the failed development methodologies of the past and provided training professionals with tools and techniques that were formerly reserved for business quality professionals. This book continues his tradition of applying successful business and technological approaches to training by providing trainers and learning professionals with a framework for applying and integrating one of today's most exciting new technologies into their training toolkit.

This book is extremely timely, as factors such as globalization, the new virtual enterprise, and the increasing use of flextime become more the norm than the exception in the workplace. *Globalization* has led to workforces that are distributed across time and space. The *virtual enterprise* now consists of alliances across a value chain, with quick-forming, quick-dissolving teams being assembled from different companies that may never meet face-to-face. *Flextime* and the rapid pace of our work lives have made it harder to meet face-to-face. All these factors have made it imperative that distributed teams find new ways to effectively collaborate, learn, and share knowledge. This workplace transformation is critical in the connected economy as a key element to attract, retain, and enable talented employees.

In a global knowledge economy, companies must also constantly increase the rate at which they improve their products and services in order to keep pace with the tempo of markets worldwide. If they hope to prosper in a rapidly changing environment, companies must learn quickly and make smart decisions consistently. To achieve these goals, organizations must leverage not only their corporate data and information assets but also, and especially, the collective knowledge of employees around the world. Organizations must sharpen their ability to enhance, shape, and focus corporate intelligence. This statement is a truism for any organization, including the training organization.

Today's office building was designed in an earlier industrial age to mimic the assembly lines that made Ford so successful, with individual knowledge workers in offices (or more recently cubicles) arranged in rows. What was a breakthrough in standardizing production was marginally useful for the exchange of information and processing of transactions. In the age before copiers and fax machines, there was an advantage to centralizing workers around the information they were processing. Now, with a distributed workforce, new ways of sharing information are required. In addition, a new generation of employees expects to receive information in new ways. Podcasting is one of the new technologies that ensures that employees obtain critical information in a just-in-time, just-enough fashion, using a medium that resonates with younger, mobile workers while also appealing to Baby Boomers.

As training moves out of the classroom and starts utilizing Web 2.0 tools, it meets the mobile lifestyle of today's employees. As a former training director, I know how difficult it is for people to find time to go to a class. During the day, training interferes with work, and people want to go home to their families in the evening. Going to training can be a real hardship on people, yet the fear of losing their technical currency is profound. Listening to a podcast during the daily commute or while traveling to a customer site is both efficient and effective.

Taking learning out of the classroom with podcasts and other distance learning options is more than just convenient. It often provides a higher-quality learning experience as well. Ness Giles is the director of operational instruction at the University of Maryland University College. The school works with about 3,000 students each semester. She is of the firm belief that the distance learning classes are superior to classroom experiences that people have.

As a former college professor and someone who has designed an end-to-end methodology that has been used in deploying over a hundred blended learning solutions for Fortune 500 corporations, I have a lot of passion for helping organizations to reduce time-to-proficiency. In working with companies both large and small that have struggled to adapt and to apply the latest technologies for their learning programs in a way that not only engages the learners, but also makes good business sense, I applaud Kaliym Islam's step-by-step approach to teaching learning professionals how to develop, deliver, and integrate podcasting into their programs in a way that balances process and the application of new technologies.

While the technology of e-learning gets most of the media attention, it can no more create a successful learning experience than a brand new school building can guarantee a great class. For knowledge workers to acquire critical thinking skills such as analysis, integration, and problem solving, and learn to apply them to real-life business situations, the instructional design and technological tools must mirror best practices of face-to-face education. Understanding technology without understanding the people who use it is useless, and as I frequently point out, today's business world is characterized by relentless change, driven by constant innovations in technology. To manage change, you must understand critical trends and their personal and organizational implications. What is needed is an expert in both IT and human nature. Kaliym Islam is exactly that.

The book you have in your hand teaches trainers and training organizations everything they need to know about developing and deploying podcasts. It will help you think in a new way about how podcasting is deployed in organizations. It will also provide you with an approach to designing instruction, utilizing podcasts that guarantee improved workplace performance, and will allow you to take an information dissemination option that was once available only to the technological elite.

Bill Bruck, Ph.D.
Founder of Q2 Learning
Falls Church, Virginia
March 2007

Preface

The world of work as we know it is forever changed. The knowledge economy requires that the most up-to-date information be available to users at any time and accessible via an unlimited number of venues. Mobile audio devices such as iPods have already revolutionized the world of music. In the near future, podcasting will revolutionize the world of training.

Here's one example of how podcasting offers an efficient training solution:

> Charles, a sales manager, has sent training representatives all over the country to explain the features of the company's new software product to current and new customers. Only a few minutes ago, the director of product development called to say that a product enhancement, a key selling feature for his sales reps, has gone into production. "Great news," says Charles. "Now I can make sure the reps have the latest product specs and speaker's notes." Charles sends a quick e-mail to the training manager. "We're all set," he writes. "Go ahead and update the podcast."
>
> The next morning, one of Charles's sales reps, who is scheduled to meet with a client at 10 a.m. to explain the features of the company's product, listens to the updated podcast while she exercises on a treadmill in her hotel's fitness center. In the taxi on the way to the meeting, she listens to the latest version of the speaking points to cover in her presentation.
>
> That night, a new employee at Charles's company is packing up his briefcase with documents about the product enhancements

to read on the commute home so he can be prepared for a marketing meeting early the next morning. "I'll never get through all these on the train," he realizes, "especially if I can't get a seat." He plugs his iPod into his computer. Within a few seconds the product information podcast has been downloaded to his device so he can learn about the enhancements while clinging to a handhold during his evening commute.

It's impossible to identify the number of podcasts among the many currently available on both public and organizational Web sites that could or should be categorized as training. The podcast directory (www.podcast.net) has cataloged over two thousand shows that would fit under this umbrella, with topics ranging from "how to give better presentations" to "effective leadership techniques." Drexel University of Philadelphia recently launched the fourth installment of its "Drexel e-Learning Minute" podcast, designed for students new to e-learning. Thousands of similar sites provide podcasts on various topics, with new ones going online every day. This growing phenomenon has launched a whole new world with opportunities both for learners and training professionals. This book was written to help you take advantage of these opportunities so that you might improve the way training is delivered in your organization and better reach the new generation of learners now entering the workforce.

Part One

THE BACKGROUND

1

TRAINING TODAY

Today's training organization faces challenges that did not exist just a few years ago. For one thing, the speed of doing business has increased. Information travels back and forth in seconds rather than days. Decisions are made quickly, and people expect quick answers to their questions.

The speed required to develop training programs to support a business has also increased. Everything seems to change more and more quickly—software applications are frequently updated, new approaches to leadership are constantly being deployed, processes and policies are constantly being revised. New regulatory and compliance rules seem to pop up every day, too. Workers need a constant flow of information and training just to keep up.

Meeting the Needs of the Workforce

The workforce has also changed. According to the U.S. Census, our workers now spend more than a hundred hours a year commuting. Not only is this new workforce more mobile, it is more decentralized—a single manager might have employees in several areas of the country, or even scattered around the globe, all of whom need to receive the same information at the same time.

These new workers are also far more technologically savvy than their parents. Having grown up with computers, cell phones, personal electronic devices, mobile audio players, and the Internet, the children of the Baby Boomers expect instant communication. Accustomed to doing more than one thing at a time, they see nothing unusual about sending and receiving instant messages, making phone calls, listening to music, reading and replying to e-mail, and writing reports all at the same time over a latte at Starbucks.

Always busy, they carry their work with them and consider downtime—the time spent waiting for an airplane or an appointment—as time in which to get something done. Yet even though they put in long hours, they never seem to have enough time. As a result, many of the traditional approaches to training don't meet their needs. It's hard for them to see the value of time spent sitting in a workshop or seminar. Even much of the e-learning that organizations have spent so much money to produce or purchase is too slow and plodding for workers' fast-paced, fluid environment. They want information delivered as quickly and efficiently as possible.

Richard Sweeny, the university librarian at New Jersey Institute of Technology, has done research on the newest generation of college students, the group he refers to as Millennials. His studies of those students born between 1979 and 1994 show that:

- This generation is the most racially and ethnically diverse in U.S. history.
- Thirty percent of the population are considered auditory learners (versus 65 percent who are visual and 5 percent who are tactile).
- They want options and customization in every aspect of their lives.
- They hate to waste time and want to learn quickly. They rarely read instructions and prefer to learn by doing and interacting.
- They want to be mobile.
- They were raised on computers and adapt faster to new technologies than any generation before them.

Thus the challenge becomes how to deliver a learning experience when and where these new learners need it, deliver it in a format that works for them, and ensure that the content is kept up-to-date. Podcasts, which make use of the electronic media that are an integral part of their environment and present information in the snippets that they prefer, offer an ideal option for addressing many of the realities of today's learning landscape.

What Is Podcasting?

The New Oxford American Dictionary defines the term *podcast* as "a digital recording of a radio broadcast or similar program, made available on the Internet for downloading to a personal audio player." According to Wikipedia, the term, a combination of "iPod" and "broadcast," was coined by Ben Hammersley in an article in *The Guardian* on February 12, 2004. Like *radio*, the term *podcast* can refer to both the content and the method of delivery.

A podcast, then, is a digital audio program, a multimedia computer file that can be downloaded to a computer, an iPod, or another device, then played or replayed on demand. Updated content and new editions can be downloaded quickly and, in some cases, automatically.

While audio (or video) on the Web is nothing new, podcasts are intriguing because they combine the benefits of being always available, portable, easy to control, automatic, and inexpensive.

Always Available

Podcasts are like radio shows on demand. They can be listened to at any time. This concept frees individuals from appointment-based listening or scheduled workshops because the program is always ready to be delivered. This aspect is especially attractive to busy professionals whose schedules are packed with meetings and who must constantly look for opportunities to learn new skills or refine the skills they already possess.

Portable

Podcasts are generally distributed using MP3 audio files. This format, with its small file size, is perfect for downloading from the Internet and transferring to portable media players. This portability further frees the trainee, who can actually take a class while traveling to and from work or while on a plane—or sitting in the airport. The portability of podcasts truly supports the concept of learning on demand.

Easy to Control

With podcasts, the listener is in control. Unlike e-mail, where the sender decides who gets a file, podcasts let the listener decide. If people subscribe to a particular training podcast series and then decide that they no longer want to take classes on that subject, they can unsubscribe, and the programs will stop coming.

Automatic

Podcasts can be downloaded automatically to the user's computer. Thus, once users have identified the types of training they would like to take and then subscribed to them, they no longer need to look for content. The content comes to them.

Inexpensive

One of the primary advantages of using podcasting for training is that it is far less expensive than most other training methods. According to *eWeek* magazine, "Getting started with podcasting is so inexpensive that it hardly makes a dent in most companies' capital budget." (The article, titled "Podcasting: An Enterprise Hit," is in the edition of October 2, 2006.)

The History of Podcasting

The concept now referred to as podcasting dates back to 2000, although the technical components were not available until the start of 2001, and it wasn't until 2003 that regular audio downloads started to show up on well-known Web sites. By that time, however, the concept had taken off—and by the end of 2004, thousands of podcasts were available.

The *pod* part of the name came about because Apple Computer's iPod digital audio player was popular when podcasting began. In fact, the use of *pod* in 2004 probably played a part in Apple's development of podcasting products and services in 2005, further linking the device and the activity in the news media. The term is really a misnomer, because podcasting doesn't require an iPod and no over-the-air broadcasting is required. Nonetheless, it has maintained its hold in the face of numerous alternatives because it just sounds right.

Today, podcasts come in all types and sizes. News organizations offer podcasts, allowing people to stay in touch with current events without opening a newspaper or watching television. Radio shows are available as podcasts. Professional organizations offer podcasts to their members on topics of mutual interest. Museums make podcasts that can be downloaded and used as audio guides to their exhibitions. Companies use podcasts to announce new products. Universities offer podcasts on academic topics. Conference presenters make podcasts for people who are unable to attend in person. Hundreds of thousands of people and organizations use podcasts to keep themselves better connected to their readers, listeners, admirers, and critics. And Apple Computer, through its iTunes Music Store, offers tens of thousands of audio and video podcasts for download.

How Podcasting Works

The most important difference between a podcast and a traditional recorded audio presentation, such as an audiotape or a radio program, has to do with the way the podcast is created and distributed.

Most podcasts are created using software that is readily available and designed specifically to record and edit the program. The

process can be as simple as recording a single voice or as complicated as producing a show with dramatization, sound effects, and
music.

Once the podcast has been created, it is placed on a Web site
with its own unique Internet address, or URL. The site might be
part of a company intranet, or it might be a site that is available to
the general public. Users can download a single podcast, or show,
or subscribe to automatically receive updates and new shows.
They can save and replay the podcasts they have downloaded
whenever they wish.

To make their podcasts accessible to users, most podcasters use
a format called RSS, an acronym for "Really Simple Syndication"
and "Rich Site Summary." The RSS *feed* is used to distribute, or
feed, a podcast to a Web server so that users can download it. RSS
feeds make it possible for the content provider, such as a trainer
or training organization, to automatically deliver updated or new
podcasts to subscribers.

For more details about the process of creating and distributing
podcasts, see Part Two.

Summary

The increasing pace of business has forced training organizations
to confront challenges that did not exist just a few years ago. More
and more there is a need to deliver learning content more quickly
(just to keep pace with the changing business environment).
Training organizations are also expected to accomplish this increased speed to market without major capital investments. Combine this reality with the new tech-savvy, multitasking, computer-
literate learners who are entering the workforce, and it is quite
obvious that there is a need for a new approach to delivering
learning content.

Podcasts are the perfect solution for this situation. These on-
demand learning objects are portable, always available, easy to
control, and inexpensive. Users can download a single podcast,

or show, or subscribe to automatically receive updates and new shows. They can also save and replay the podcasts they have downloaded whenever they wish. Some might compare podcasts to an older and more common concept of posting audio or video training on the Web. The difference, however, is the use of RSS. RSS feeds make it possible for the content provider, such as a trainer or training organization, to automatically deliver updated or new podcasts to subscribers. This relatively new technology only began showing up on Web sites in 2003 but is quickly becoming the learning option of choice for many of the Millennial generation.

2

PODCASTING FOR TRAINING

For training organizations, podcasting has the potential to be one of the most exciting technologies to emerge in recent history. It also has the potential to be one of the most disruptive.

Podcasting can allow any trainer or training organization (regardless of the size or budget) to present ideas, concepts, and policies to a target audience or to the general public anywhere in the world. The minimal investment required to begin podcasting levels the playing field between large multinational training organizations and one-person shops.

Podcasting can also be disruptive. As I write, it has no rules and no regulating bodies. Podcasts can be a minute long or an hour long. They have no set formats and no industry-recognized best practices. In fact, virtually anyone with a microphone and a computer can begin to produce and publish podcasts. This lack of standards, rules, and best practices creates the potential for years of infighting (among training professionals) to get agreement on how podcasting fits into a trainer's tool kit, and how to best develop podcasts. This type of infighting can potentially be damaging to the relationship between trainers and their business stakeholders. Business stakeholders already tend to have less than a favorable impression of training organizations. Perceived confusion or inconsistency on how to develop and deploy podcasts might further damage this fragile relationship. Taking all of this into account, however, podcasting as a training option is a reality and will forever change the life of training organizations.

Benefits of Using Podcasts for Training

As mentioned earlier, podcasts offer many benefits as a training option:

- As a general rule, podcasts can be produced much more quickly than regular video programs, even when they contain video material. This quicker production allows you to get media-rich content to the people who need it in a more timely manner.
- The delivery method allows trainers to get people a message at the same time across a vast world where everyone is working virtually. Whether it's just-in-time training on a new product or teaching employees the new approach for filing expense reports, this medium allows trainers to reach a huge number of people quickly.
- Just-in-time media like podcasts that can be reviewed more than once have been shown to have positive effects on students who are reviewing for tests.
- Podcasting allows training to be delivered on a flexible time schedule.
- Learners can listen to the podcast whenever they want, and wherever they may be.

What's Next?

The adoption and practical application of podcasting as a training option seems to be inevitable. As the technology becomes more commonplace in the larger environment, it seems natural that the training world will follow. Early in 2006, Forrester Research projected just 700,000 households in the United States would use podcasting that year. That number, however, would grow to 12.3 million households by 2010. (See http://blogs.forrester.com/charleneli/2006/04/forrester_podca.html.)

To give some context, the expectation of MP3 adoption was for about 11 million households in the United States in 2006, growing to 34.5 million households by 2010. This means that in four years about a third of MP3 owners will be listening to podcasts on those devices. Podcasting will get easier and the content will get better. The bottom line is that people are adopting podcasting as a listening option even more quickly than they adopted the use of MP3 players themselves. Just as it is common now to see individuals with earplugs listening to portable music devices as they commute, garden, or work out, it will more quickly become commonplace for individuals to listen to podcasts.

It's not surprising that learning professionals are discovering the advantages of podcasting as a training tool. Podcasts are relatively easy to create without high-priced equipment. They make it possible to deliver content on demand, allowing users to access the information wherever and whenever they choose. Used in conjunction with other forms of learning, podcasts can add value to any organization's training efforts.

Here are a few examples of trailblazers who have already begun to take advantage of this new medium:

- IBM has been using podcasting to deliver information to its employees internally, and is now publishing real-time updates for investors, so they can keep up with IBM's take on the future and direction of business and IT. The new series, titled "IBM and the future of . . ." began with a podcast on IBM and the future of driving.

- The "Negotiating Tip of the Week" podcast series, featuring Dr. Josh Weiss from the Program on Negotiation at Harvard, was downloaded more than 280,000 times between April 2005 and January 2006. The popularity of the series also convinced Kathleen Gilroy, founder of the Otter Group, to offer custom podcasts for clients. The venture has proved extremely successful—her $15,000 investment soon led to more than $100,000 in receipts from sales of custom podcasts.

- The Otter Group's latest venture, "Everybody's a CEO," helps businesspeople go "Back to School 2.0" and learn the importance of (and how to implement) blogs, RSS, podcasts, and a "Personal Learning Network" as a form of interactive accountability.

- Herbalife, maker of nutritional supplements, is creating podcast training programs for its distributors around the globe. The company has already given away more than a million iPods to its employees.

- In 2006 General Motors (GM) launched Fast Lane radio as an offshoot of its Fast Lane blog. This radio-style podcast about GM's cars, featuring interviews with top executives in design, engineering, and marketing, gives car enthusiasts and the general public an inside scoop on the largest auto company in the world.

- Drexel University of Philadelphia produces a podcast called the "Drexel e-Learning Minute," which helps students new to e-learning address various issues and provides the prospective online learner with tools for success.

- Capital One, a financial services provider, hands out iPods as standard equipment for employees who enroll in targeted training programs and makes podcasts available on the company's intranet and corporate Web site. The driver behind Capital One's use of podcasts is a vexing deficit—not in dollars and cents—but in time.

- Pal's Restaurants, based in Kingsport, Tennessee, uses audio and video podcasts to train all its restaurant employees. According to CEO Thom Crosby, "Podasts give us the capability to better train today's generation of employees. They can watch or listen to a thirty- or sixty-second podcast right at their work station."

The potential of podcasting as a learning tool is virtually limitless. To make the best use of this tool, however, trainers and training organizations need to understand what this dynamic new medium can accomplish, what its limitations are, and how to integrate podcasts with more traditional forms of training.

Podcasting: An Appropriate Training Option?

With all that podcasting has to offer as a revolutionary new training medium, it's important to remember that—like any new technology—it will not meet every need. Training professionals should always pause and think about whether podcasting will work in their specific situation before they jump in and embrace it.

Perhaps the most important point to keep in mind is that podcasting cannot replace all the other types of training that an organization offers. Like a radio program or an audiotape, a podcast provides information in a one-way format. Because podcasting does not allow for interactivity and feedback, it is more like a lecture or an explanation than a training session, so it is best suited to providing just-in-time information about topics that are subject to frequent change and for expanding on and reinforcing what people learn in seminars, workshops, self-study, and e-learning programs.

Still, when used with other training methods, podcasting can be a very useful tool for achieving your training objectives. It can help you with the following goals:

- *Reinforce training.* As mentioned earlier, 30 percent of the population are auditory learners. Podcasts are excellent ways to help those people retain information they have learned through other methods. For example, podcasts that provide summaries of key learning points or lectures allow people to review the material as often as needed.

- *Supplement training.* Not everything can be covered in a workshop or seminar. Podcasts can offer supplementary lectures, interviews, or case studies that build on what people learn in a classroom or other training program. Podcasts can also substitute for between-class reading assignments.

- *Follow up on training.* Once people have participated in a training program on a specific topic, podcasts can be used to provide additional training. For example, podcasts can be used to deliver updated content on the topic and suggest ways the learner can continue to apply the learning.

- *Provide information to people who cannot attend a training session.* Podcasts can provide the text of lecture material, highlights of key points, and other content for people who need the information provided in a workshop or seminar but are unable to attend.

- *Help people prepare for tests.* In many industries, people need to take tests or certification examinations. Podcasts can be used to help them prepare by providing a convenient way to review the information they have learned in workshops, seminars, and self-study programs.

- *Replace content-only portions of training programs.* Classroom-based training, online training programs, and self-study materials all include portions that simply deliver information. That information can be delivered via podcast, freeing up valuable training time for activities that require interaction, practice, and feedback.

Selecting the Best Training Options

To choose the best option or options for a specific situation and objectives, it is important to think about the training requirements. Table 2.1 shows some of the factors to consider.

Table 2.1 Training Options Chart

Requirement	Podcasting	Self-Paced or E-learning	Live Instructor-Led Web-Based Training	Classroom Training
Content requires frequent updates	X			
Needs quick deployment	X		X	
Requires interaction (simulations)		X	X	X
Requires testing		X	X	X
Requires minimal cost to develop	X			
Requires minimal investment to begin	X			X
Must be just in time	X			
Must cover dynamic (frequently changing) topics	X		X	
Must have flexible listening options	X		X	
Requires "show me" simulations	X	X	X	
New content must be pushed to learners	X			
Requires speed to market	X		X	
Must be portable	X			
Must be controlled by the user	X			

Summary

Podcasting holds great potential as a training option, but it also has some pitfalls. One pitfall is the lack of universally accepted standards, rules, or best practices associated with training podcasts. This condition creates an opening for a further disconnect between training professionals and the businesses that they serve.

As a training option, however, podcasting seems to be here to stay; there's no turning back. The adoption of podcasting is occurring even faster than the adoption of MP3 players, and trailblazing organizations like IBM, Drexel University, and General Motors have already adopted this medium as part of their training solutions.

Although podcasting has a great deal to offer for use in the training space, it is not a silver bullet. Revolutionary as it is, it's important to remember that, like any new technology, it will not meet every need. Training professionals must always consider whether podcasting is the appropriate training solution for specific situations. In the next chapter I explore some of the legal issues that you should consider when thinking about podcasting as a training option.

3

LEGAL ISSUES TO CONSIDER WHEN CREATING PODCASTS

Podcasting is fun and exciting and speaks to the needs of today's work environment and today's learner. The podcast structure is flexible and allows for maximum creativity on the part of the podcaster.

That said, with the flexibility and the freedom comes some very real accountability. Whenever you want to use third-party material in a podcast, you must obtain the necessary rights and permissions—and that applies to anything that has not been created by you or your organization. Using material created by others raises complex legal issues.

The primary legal issues that affect podcasts are related to copyright, publicity rights, and trademarks.

Copyright Issues

Copyright law applies to creative and expressive works, including performances, scripts, interviews, musical works, and sound recordings. Under current U.S. copyright law, copyright attaches automatically to creative, expressive works once they have been written down or recorded. Thus, when you come across such a work that you would like to include in a podcast, you should as a general rule assume that it is protected by copyright.

Copyright law gives the owner of the copyright the exclusive right to control certain activities in relation to the work. For example, copyright owners can control whether another person makes a copy of their work, makes changes to their work, distributes it to the public, or performs it in public. Anyone who wishes to do any of the protected acts in relation to that work must obtain prior permission from the copyright owner.

When creating a podcast, you need permission to use a copyrighted work if you wish to do any of the following:

- Copy the work to include in your podcast.
- Adapt or change the work to include it in your podcast.
- Make the work available as part of your podcast for transmission to members of the public.
- Authorize members of the public to make a copy of your podcast (which contains the copyrighted work) and to use it.

What makes the legal issues somewhat difficult for podcasters is that there is no firm rule about how much of a work may be used or copied to avoid these concerns—copyright can be invoked if an entire piece is recorded verbatim, which seems obvious, but it can also be invoked if the work is changed dramatically and the podcast is only loosely based on the text. Thus, to avoid possible copyright infringement, it is good practice to ask for permission before including copyrighted material in any form, except in the instances I discuss next.

When You Do Not Need Permission to Use Material Created by Others

You do not need to secure the separate permission of the provider of a work when any of the following conditions apply:

- The specific material you are using was never protected by copyright.
- The material was protected by copyright but is now in the public domain.

- The U.S. government created the material.
- You are making a "fair use" of the work.
- You wish to make more than a "fair use" of the work and the work is under a Creative Commons license that authorizes the intended use.

When the Material Is Not Protected by Copyright

Although an entire textual work may be protected by copyright, elements of that work may not be subject to the exclusive rights of the copyright owner. Copyright law only protects the creative expression, and it is a general principle of copyright law that copyright does not extend to ideas or facts. For example, you could discuss the ideas and theories that are presented in a blog, an editorial, or another opinion piece without asking the permission of the author or publisher (although you might want to consider anti-defamation laws before engaging in especially harsh criticism of a theory or an author). Discussion of factual events reported in a newspaper—such as facts about historical or current events—can be included in a podcast without obtaining permission from the copyright owner or the newspaper.

Material in the Public Domain

Work that is in the public domain can be used without obtaining permission of the original author or copyright owner. In the United States, a work is considered in the public domain if the copyright term has expired, if copyright protection for that work was not maintained, or if the author or copyright owner has dedicated the work to the public domain.

As a general rule, in the United States copyright will only have expired if the work was published before 1923. Works published in 1923 or later have had their term of copyright protection extended and so will not join the public domain until 2019 or later unless copyright protection was not properly maintained—and recognizing an unmaintained copyright is usually too hard or too risky to be worth trying.

U.S. Government Works

Works that are created by U.S. government employees or officers as part of their official duties are not protected by copyright. Similarly, federal and state statutes and judicial opinions are not protected by copyright. However, works created by state and local officials and employees are usually copyright-protected. Similarly, material created by private persons who are commissioned by the federal government to prepare a work may be protected by copyright.

If you incorporate government works into a podcast, you should consider including a statement that identifies which portions of your podcast are protected by copyright and which are U.S. government works. This is important because it tells people which works they can freely use and repurpose. It removes the ability for someone to argue that he or she did not have proper notice of the copyrighted status of the work.

Fair Use

A "fair use" is copying any protected material (texts, sounds, images, and so on) for a limited and "transformative" purpose, such as criticizing, commenting, parodying, news reporting, or teaching. Under the U.S. copyright laws, fair use "is not an infringement of copyright." Limited copying of protected materials is therefore acceptable for training podcasts if the copied material is being used to teach a topic. There are limits, however. For example, short excerpts from my book *Developing and Measuring Training The Six Sigma Way* (Pfeiffer, 2006) may be read as part of a podcast and then discussed under fair use—but someone could not claim fair use if an entire chapter were quoted.

Creative Commons License

Creative Commons licenses signal to the public how a piece of work may be used without violating copyright laws. Here are some popular types of Creative Commons license:

- NoDerivatives: This license requires that any copy of the work you make is verbatim, with no changes made to the original work.
- NonCommercial: This license specifies that you cannot make money from the work. In other words, you could not sell the podcast for a profit.
- ShareAlike: This license requires that, if you make a derivative work of a Creative Commons–licensed piece of content, you license your own podcast under the same or similar Creative Commons license terms. That is, if you take a Creative Commons–licensed book and read it aloud as part of your podcast, your podcast must then provide a Creative Commons license that contains the same license elements.

Besides the specific limits defined by the type, if you use a Creative Commons–licensed work in your podcast, you must include the title of the work and keep intact any copyright notices that accompany the work.

Publicity Rights

Publicity rights allow individuals to control how their voice, image, or likeness is used in public for commercial purposes. These rights are relevant to training podcasts because in creating a podcast a trainer may conduct audio or video interviews or even produce other spoken or visual content. When transmitting voices or images of anyone other than a member of your own organization, you might need to get permission from those individuals.

A claim of right to publicity generally arises when a podcast uses another person's image, likeness, or voice without consent and for commercial purposes. This means that if you use someone's image, likeness, or voice to advertise or solicit sales of a podcast, you will need the individual's consent. For example, if you were to create a podcast discussing the work of Dr. Donald Kirkpatrick (who developed the four-level approach to evaluating training) and you used Dr. Kirkpatrick's image to help sell the podcast, Dr. Kirkpatrick might have a claim of publicity rights—especially if your podcast was competing with one of his own.

An individual must have suffered some injury in order to have a valid claim of right to publicity. The first amendment of the U.S. Constitution allows uses of a public figure's name or likeness so long as it is done in a truthful way and does not imply a false endorsement of a person or product by the public figure. Right of publicity, however, is governed by state law, which means that it can vary from state to state. For example, in California, a person filing a lawsuit would need to show that a podcast creator used the plaintiff's name, voice, photograph, or likeness in order to advertise, sell, or solicit the podcast without the individual's consent. But California law includes an important exception: In situations in which the name, voice, signature, photograph, or likeness of an individual is used "in connection with any news, public affairs, or sports broadcast or accounts, or any political campaign," consent is not required.

Relevant Trademark Law

Trademark law is designed to protect consumers from being misled or deceived as to the source of goods and services, or the endorsement, sponsorship, or affiliation of one good or service with another. Another way of stating this is that trademark law works to ensure that individuals can rely on particular branding to equate to certain product features. Even if you are Lee McDonald, for example, you still cannot use the name "McDonald's" and apply it in such a way as to suggest that your podcasts come from McDonald's Restaurants or are endorsed by or affiliated with that company.

While there might be little risk that you or your organization would associate someone else's trademark with your podcast, trademark law can be implicated in what is done or said in relation to your podcast in other ways. Generally, a trademark can be violated in two ways: by direct infringement and by dilution.

Direct Infringement

Direct infringement occurs when you use someone else's trademark (often a competitor's trademark) in a way that is "likely to cause consumer confusion" as to the source, affiliation, or sponsorship between you and the trademark owner. This might occur if you use a trademark to describe your podcast, and the trademark owner thinks your podcast is so closely related to its product or service that a listener might conclude that the podcast comes from or is endorsed by the trademark owner, even though this is not the case. For example, if you named your training podcast "The IBM Approach to Six Sigma Training," IBM might well send you a cease-and-desist letter. But if the podcast was called "The IBM Approach to Gourmet Cooking," there would be less risk of an infringement claim, because people are unlikely to think that the well-known computer company was sponsoring a podcast about being a chef. But you wouldn't be risk-free—read on.

Dilution

Dilution can occur if the character of the trademark becomes clouded by an unwanted association, either through *tarnishment,* which occurs when a famous mark is used to promote a product that is considered offensive, or through *blurring,* which means the use of a famous trademark causes consumers to blur the two companies in their minds (for example, naming your podcast the "Nike Trash Collection Discussion Group").

In a dilution claim, a trademark owner must prove actual dilution, not merely the likelihood of dilution. Dilution does not occur from a *nominative* or informational use of a trademark, such as a critical review, or what is known as a *descriptive* use of a trademark, such as using it in a sentence to discuss Nike footwear or the Nike Corporation.

A Final Word on Legal Issues

As a general rule, if the podcast incorporates text that has been written by someone else, you will need the expressed and specific permission of the person who owns copyright in that material. Written works do not have to be full of flourish and artistic merit, like novels and poetry, to qualify for copyright protection. Textual works need have only minimal creativity to attract copyright protection, so most works that are committed to paper (or computer) are likely to be protected by copyright. In addition to legal issues that might occur as a result of copyright laws, podcasters must also consider trademark issues as well as publicity issues.

Summary

There is no question that podcasts speak to the needs of today's learner. The flexible structure of podcasting allows for maximum creativity, and this medium addresses the issues of today's work environment. With this flexibility and freedom, however, comes some very real accountability. Some very serious legal issues must be considered when you embark upon podcasting.

If any podcast that you are creating will contain anything that has not been created by you or your organization, you must obtain the necessary rights and permissions. The primary legal issues that affect podcasts are related to copyright, publicity rights, and trademarks. Copyright law applies to creative and expressive works, including performances, scripts, interviews, musical works, and sound recordings. Publicity rights allow individuals to control how their voice, image, or likeness is used in public for commercial purposes, and trademark law is designed to protect consumers from being misled or deceived as to the source of goods and services, or an endorsement.

4

HARDWARE AND SOFTWARE REQUIREMENTS FOR PODCASTING

One of the benefits of using podcasting for training is the minimal investment required. Your training department probably has what it needs to develop podcasts with virtually no additional investment. On the other hand, if you want to deliver podcasts with broadcast-quality sound and video, the department could spend thousands of dollars securing the proper equipment.

At minimum, creating and distributing an audio podcast requires a computer with a broadband Internet connection, a microphone, and a sound editing software package. For a podcast that includes video, you also need a FireWire video camera and video editing software. I discuss FireWire later in this chapter.

Hardware Requirements and Options

Depending on the complexity of the podcast and the quality necessary, many factors influence the choice of hardware and software to record, edit, mix, and distribute your podcasts. This section introduces you to some of the hardware that you might need to use to produce a podcast, including microphones, pop filters, headphones, mixers, cables, and connectors. It will also describe different audio and video recording software.

Computer

The first piece of podcasting gear required is a computer. Any modern computer will do for making a podcast, and you can use either a Mac or a PC. There are, however, some benefits to using a Mac. If your Mac runs OS X, it is already equipped with hardware sufficient to create podcasts and a suite of software that supports podcast development, eliminating the need to download, install, or purchase any third-party software.

Typically, the most demanding activity that any computer needs to accomplish to create a podcast is the recording and processing of audio or video files. The more RAM (Read-Only Memory) your computer has, the faster it will operate when accomplishing these tasks.

To record and process audio files, you'll need a minimum of 512 MB of RAM. These days, most computers are shipped with at least 512 MB of RAM—but more would be good to have. Recording and processing video requires additional processing power and additional memory. If your organization intends to use video in your training podcasts, you should consider adding as much RAM as the computer can support. As a general rule, you typically need twice the amount of RAM for video as you would require for smooth audio processing.

Your computer will also need at least two or three gigabytes of free hard drive space for saving audio and video files. Even if your organization plans to archive the audio and video, compress the audio and video, or save the files to a network location, your local computer should still have several gigabytes of space available. If you plan to archive the audio without compressing it to MP3, then make sure you have several more gigabytes of space. It is probably also a good idea to invest in an external hard drive or some other external storage device to store and archive sound and video files.

The computer you use to develop your podcast will also need a sound card, speakers, and jacks for a microphone and headphones. These days most computers come with these components. If you are using an older model, you must determine whether you are better off adding the additional hardware or purchasing a new computer.

Requirements for a PC

- Windows XP or greater
- At least 512 MB of RAM (the more RAM, the faster the computer will operate)
- Two or three gigabytes of free hard drive space for saving audio and video files
- A sound card
- Speakers
- An external microphone
- Line in/out or Mic/Headphone jacks

Requirements for a Mac

- A Mac running OS X
- At least 512 MB of RAM (increased RAM means increased performance)
- 2–3 gigabytes of free hard drive space for saving audio and video files
- An external microphone

Microphones

Many people would argue that the microphone is the most important piece of hardware associated with podcast development. Although most computers now come equipped with internal microphones, the quality of the recording made using those microphones is not good enough for a podcast, especially one that will be used for training. Your podcast will be more successful if you use a good external microphone.

The microphone you select depends on the type of podcast you are making as well as the situation in which you will be doing the recording. Factors to consider include whether you are recording only one voice or several voices, where you will be making the recording (in a studio, in an open office, outdoors), and how much money you have to spend.

Microphones differ in the way they capture sound waves and in their pickup patterns—the direction from which they pick up sounds. Here are brief descriptions of the differences.

Sound Wave Capture. These days, microphones capture sounds in one of two basic ways. You can choose between dynamic microphones and condenser microphones.

Dynamic Microphones. Dynamic microphones use wire coils and a magnet to create the audio signal. A diaphragm is attached to the coil, and as sound waves hit the diaphragm, they move the coil back and forth past the magnet. This generates an electric current that travels through the microphone cable to the other equipment in the audio chain, where it can be saved as a recording or sent to a device such as a loudspeaker or set of headphones that then converts the electric signal back into sound waves.

Dynamic microphones have few moving parts. They tend to be durable and rugged. They generate their own current and therefore do not require an external power source. As a result, a dynamic microphone is an excellent choice if what you need is a durable general-purpose microphone. Figure 4.1 shows the cross-section of a dynamic microphone.

Condenser Microphones. Condenser microphones produce an audio signal when the sound waves hitting the diaphragm cause two plates in a small capacitor to vibrate. This vibration creates variations in the voltage between the plates. When the plates are close together, a charge current occurs. When they are farther apart, a discharge current occurs. The variations in the electrical

Figure 4.1 Dynamic Microphone Cross-Section

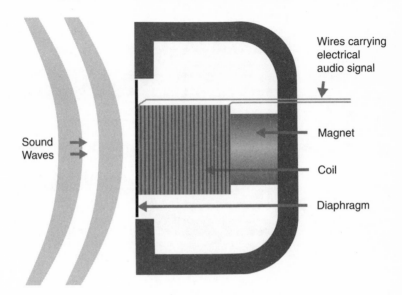

Wires carrying
electrical
audio signal

Sound
Waves

Magnet

Coil

Diaphragm

current are reinterpreted as sound waves by the receiving electrical equipment.

Since they require voltage across the capacitor, condenser microphones require power from a battery or another external power source.

Condenser microphones are sensitive, very responsive, and create a much stronger signal than dynamic microphones. This stronger signal makes them more attractive for studio work or for podcasts where you need to pick up the subtleties in a voice. Condenser microphones are, however, less durable than dynamic microphones. Figure 4.2 shows the cross-section of a condenser microphone.

Pickup Pattern. Just as microphones differ in the way they capture sound waves, they also differ in the direction from which they pick up sounds. Here, you have three options: omnidirectional, unidirectional, and bidirectional.

Figure 4.2 Condenser Microphone Cross-Section

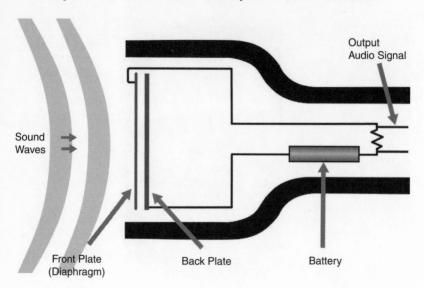

Omnidirectional Microphones. Omnidirectional microphones pick up sound from all directions. They are best suited for record-ing more than one or two people at a time with a single micro-phone. However, these microphones also pick up all the sound around those people. Any other sounds (other voices, ringing phones, rustling paper, music, or whatever) in the area where the recording is taking place may make the resulting recording sound unfocused, so the podcast will be difficult to follow. Figure 4.3 shows the pickup pattern of an omnidirectional microphone. The dark band around the entire outside region of the pickup area indicates that sound is picked up from all directions.

Unidirectional Microphones. Unidirectional microphones pick up sounds from only one direction, so they are excellent when you need to isolate specific sounds, such as the voices of two people talking. Unidirectional microphones come in two types: cardioid and hypercardioid.

Cardioid implies that the microphone picks up sounds pre-dominantly from the front, but with some pickup from the sides.

Figure 4.3 Pickup Pattern of Omnidirectional Microphone

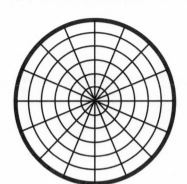

This is a good option for recording podcasts in a studio because, while the microphone isolates the speaker's voice, it gives some flexibility for side-to-side movement while speaking. For example, the speaker can shift position a little without affecting the voice level.

One disadvantage of cardioid microphones, however, is that they tend to suffer from something called the *proximity effect,* meaning that the microphone becomes more sensitive to low frequency sounds as the sound source moves closer. Thus, if the speaker is positioned within a few inches of a cardioid microphone, the resulting recording may be subject to excessive lows or "boominess." Also, when you use cardioid microphones for a roving reporter type of interview, you're apt to get a distracting whooshing sound as the microphone is passed back and forth.

Figure 4.4 shows an example of the pickup pattern of a cardioid microphone. Notice that the defined area focuses mostly on the front and slightly on the sides.

If your podcast is going to consist of a live interview and you are only using one microphone, a cardioid microphone is probably not the right choice. You can overcome this problem and use a cardioid microphone if you capture the voices of the interviewer

Figure 4.4 Pickup Pattern of Cardioid Microphone

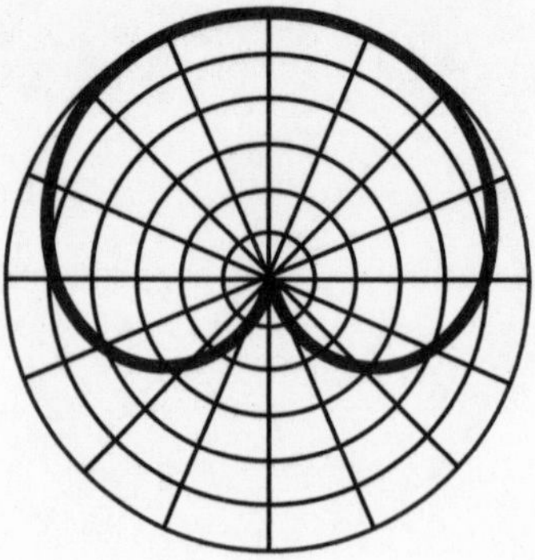

and the interviewee separately. In other words, first have the interviewer record all the questions, then pass the microphone to the interviewee to record all the answers. The recorded clips could later be organized so that it sounds as though the interviewee had been responding to each question in order.

Hypercardioid is a more extreme version of the cardioid principle. This type of microphone, which is typically long and thin, rejects almost all sounds outside of its pickup pattern. These types of microphones tend to be used in the movie industry to record dialogue. One challenge in using hypercardioid microphones for podcasting is that they reject so much sound that the resulting recording can sound cold and unnatural. Figure 4.5 shows the pickup pattern of a hypercardioid microphone.

Bidirectional Microphones. Bidirectional microphones, which have a double cardioid pattern, are relatively unpopular. As the name implies, bidirectional microphones have a pickup pattern that captures the sound from both the front and back of the microphone, with slight pickup on either side. Bidirectional microphones are a good choice for a two-person podcast, because they make it unnecessary to pass a microphone back and forth. They

Figure 4.5 Pickup Pattern of Hypercardioid Microphone

should, however, be used only in a studio setting and then only if you have a good reason not to use two separate microphones.

Figure 4.6 shows the pickup pattern of a bidirectional microphone.

Microphone Cost Considerations. A decent entry-level microphone can be purchased for as little as about $100, while a top-of-the-line model might run $4,000. Professional-grade microphones tend to be in the $300 to $400 range. If you spend less than $100 for a microphone, you will probably be disappointed.

Figure 4.6 Pickup Pattern of Bidirectional Microphone

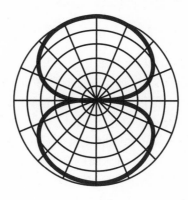

The sound quality and durability of models in that price range don't warrant the investment. Although it is seldom necessary to buy the most expensive microphone, a good microphone can greatly increase the quality of your podcast. The microphone is the first step in the portal to listeners. Just as a bad camera lens can distort a photograph, a bad microphone can ruin the learner's audio experience.

Pop Filter

A pop filter is a noise protection filter for microphones. It serves to reduce popping and hissing sounds in recorded speech and singing that tend to show up when letters like "p" hit a microphone. Pop filters are normally composed of an acoustically semitransparent material such as woven nylon stretched over a circular frame, and they often include a clamp and a flexible mounting bracket. Although a pop filter is not required to make a podcast, it can increase the quality of the audio.

Pop filters come in two types: a foam version that fits snugly over the microphone, and a screen version, that is, a shield suspended between the speaker and the microphone. A cheap pop shield can be made from material from tights or stockings stretched over a piece of wire such as a bent coat hanger.

Figure 4.7 is an example of a shield-style pop filter.

Headphones

Headphones are essential for making podcasts. Some would argue that they are second in importance to the microphone. You will use headphones not only while recording your podcasts but also while editing them, so it's important to get comfortable ones.

You have a great many headphone styles and brands to choose from, ranging in price from as little as $20 to professional-grade headphones than cost more than $100.

Figure 4.7 Pop Filter

Headset

Headsets are convenient for podcasting because they combine microphone and headphones. The cable from the headset has two plugs, one for the microphone and one for the headphones. This setup works best if the jacks on the computer are right next to each other because it makes it easier to connect and disconnect both the headphone and microphone components. The disadvantage of using a headset is that the quality of the attached microphone tends to be low.

Mixer

An optional piece of hardware that can be helpful in podcast development is a mixer: an electronic device for combining and changing the level, tone, and dynamics of audio signals. Mixers allow for multiple inputs and give the user independent control over the various sound inputs as they are combined in the audio chain. For example, with a mixer, you can use multiple microphones and set each to a different volume level, which is helpful if the podcast has several participants and some naturally speak louder than others. You should also use a mixer if you will be incorporating music or other sound effects that will be brought in via sources such as CD players or live musical instruments.

Some podcasters don't use mixers. Instead, they record directly to their computers and attempt to have the computer accomplish the work that mixers were intended to do. However, if you have any need for multiple inputs, a mixer is a good investment.

Since the podcasts will most likely be recorded using the combination of a computer and a mixer, it must be noted that many computers do not come with the "perfect" audio inputs needed for recording. It is therefore important to be aware of how the mixer will be connected to the computer. Some mixers come with connectors built right in. Others require additional assistance.

A mixer suitable for podcasting can range in price from around $60 to close to $700.

Figure 4.8 is a picture of a mixer.

Cables and Connectors

Creating podcasts may require the use of various cables and connectors. Which ones you need depends on the equipment you're

Figure 4.8 Sample Mixer

using and the type of podcast you're making. After showing you some of the various types of connectors that might be used, in this section I explain how they are used to connect the various pieces of hardware together.

RCA Connector. RCA connectors, also referred to as *phono* connectors, are commonly used in the audio and video market. The name "RCA" derives from the Radio Corporation of America, which introduced the design in the early 1940s to allow phonograph players to be connected to radios. Most people have seen RCA connectors when they needed to attach turntables, tape decks, and CD players to amplifiers or receivers, or to connect DVD players to television sets. For podcasting, this type of connector is used to connect a device that has audio and video to a mixer.

RCA connectors are color-coded: yellow for composite video, red for the right channel, and white or black for the left channel of stereo audio. This trio (or pair) of jacks can be found on the back of almost all audio and video equipment. Connections are made by pushing the cable's plug into the jack on the mixer.

Figure 4.9 shows a typical RCA connector.

Figure 4.9 RCA Connector

Phone Jack. The *phone* in "phone jack" does not refer to telephones but rather to headphones and microphones. These $\frac{1}{4}$-inch jacks are commonly used with guitars and headphones and sometimes on communication equipment such as microphone inputs and cassette recorders. They are also found on personal computer sound cards for

- Line in (stereo)
- Line out (stereo)
- Headphones/loudspeaker out (stereo)
- Microphone input

Phone jacks are used for mono and stereo signals to connect hardware such as headphones and microphones to a mixer. Figure 4.10 shows various types of phone jacks.

Figure 4.10 Phone Jacks

Mini Plug. The $\frac{1}{8}$-inch mini plug is a smaller version of the TRS phone jack. TS or mono versions of the same connector are also used as headphone input-output devices.

Channel Insert Cable. A channel insert cable is a special Y–shaped cable used to connect effects processors to a mixer. A channel cable isn't the only way to accomplish this, but it is probably the easiest. Figure 4.11 shows a typical channel insert cable.

Figure 4.11 Channel Insert Cable

XLR Connector. An XLR connector is a rugged professional-grade hookup between the microphones and the mixer. These connectors carry a balanced signal that is cleaner and stronger than the signal carried by the $\frac{1}{4}$-inch TRS phone jack. If you have the option of using either a phone jack or an XLR connector for your microphones, choose the XLR connector. Figure 4.12 is a typical XLR connector.

Figure 4.12 XLR Connector

USB. Originally designed to replace the multiple parallel ports and serial connectors on computers, Universal Serial Bus (USB) is now commonplace on video game consoles, PDAs, portable DVD and media players, cell phones, and many other devices. It is often used for connecting computers with microphones, mixers, and audio devices, so there is a good chance that you will be using this type of connection at least some of the time as you prepare your podcasts. Figure 4.13 shows a typical USB connector.

Figure 4.13 USB Connector

FireWire/IEEE 1394. FireWire is used to connect computers with video cameras, external hard drives, webcams, and even audio mixers. FireWire is a proprietary name Apple Computer uses for the IEEE 1394 interface. It is also known as i.Link or IEEE 1394.

Although created by Apple, FireWire is now a personal computer (and digital audio and digital video) serial bus interface standard. It offers high-speed communications and synchronized real-time data services. Many computers intended for home or professional audio/video use, including all Apple, Dell, and Sony computers currently produced, have built-in FireWire ports. FireWire offers fast, clean, all-digital transfers of audio to a computer.

Figure 4.14 shows an example of a FireWire connector.

Figure 4.14 FireWire Connector

Audio Interfaces and Sound Cards

Headphones, microphones, cables, and phone jacks all ultimately need to be connected to your computer. This connection is typically handled via the use of an audio interface or sound card, or both.

Audio Interface. If you are using a mixer, you will need a way to get the audio from the mixer into the computer. You might be able to plug the mixer directly into the computer, but it's not always that simple. While most computers come equipped with some type of audio connection, a dedicated, high-quality audio interface is the best solution in the long run.

A USB interface acts as a bridge between the audio equipment and the computer. The audio equipment plugs into one end of the interface, and the interface plugs into the USB port on the computer. Audio interface devices can range in cost from around $40 to well over $1,000.

Sound Card. While an audio interface is an external bridge between the computer and the audio equipment, a sound card is installed directly into the body of the computer, thus extending the audio capabilities of the computer. All computers now come with sound cards installed. The card includes digital-to-analog converters for audio outputs and analog-to-digital converters for audio inputs. The inputs and outputs tend to be mounted on the card itself, giving the user convenient connectors right on the back or side of the computer.

Phone Patches and Digital Hybrids

If your podcast will contain interviews, you might need to talk with someone who is in a remote location. One way to accomplish that is to record a telephone interview, then patch the audio into your computer or mixer. This can be accomplished by using either a simple and inexpensive phone patch or an expensive but very professional digital hybrid.

Phone Patch. A phone patch is a simple piece of hardware that takes the sound from a telephone line and sends it directly to a computer or mixer. With a phone patch, the signal is not processed in any way, so every sound coming through the phone will be recorded—the caller's voice, the interviewer's voice, and possibly any background sounds as well. Phone patches run around $30.

Digital Hybrid. Depending on the situation and your budget, a digital hybrid might offer a better way of capturing the voice of the person in the remote location. A digital hybrid is an expensive piece of professional hardware that strips out the voice of the host and leaves the caller's voice in isolation. The hybrid is connected to the mixer so that a microphone can be used to capture the host's part of the conversation, while the caller's voice is captured on a separate channel or track. For example, you might have the microphone recording your part of the conversation on track five and the hybrid audio (the audio of the remote caller) on track three. Digital hybrids are most productive if you use a mixer. The cost tends to start at around $1000.

Setting Up the Hardware

Once you have obtained all the hardware needed to develop your podcast, you have to put it together. The good news is that this is a relatively simple process. The specifics might be slightly different depending on how many different pieces of hardware you are using, but the audio signals always flow in the direction away from the mouth and toward the recording device. Here is a standard configuration using a mixer:

- Connect the microphone to the mixer's microphone inputs using XLR connectors.
- Connect external sound sources like CD players or musical keyboards to the mixer's line in inputs using phone plugs.
- If you're also using a gate (discussed in Chapter Eight), use special channel insert cables to connect the equipment to the channel insert jacks. The sound will then flow from the mixer to the external boxes and then back into the mixer.
- Connect a cable from the phone jack to the "main out" of the audio interface that is plugged into the computer or recording device.
- Monitor the sound using headphones plugged into the headphone jack on the mixer.

Monitoring sound during podcast recording should always take place through headphones that are plugged into a mixer, not a computer. Monitoring sound through a computer headphone jack will feed the sound back to your ears a split second or two after the sound actually occurs. For example, you might say a word and then a fraction of a second later you hear the same word in the headphones. This triggers a *latency* effect, where your brain is so busy trying to get your ears and mouth in synch that you tend to slur your words. It might be tempting to monitor sound through the computer headphone jack, but the best advice is to stick with the equipment that was actually designed for the job.

Basic Podcasting Software

In general, software for podcast creation falls into one of four categories: tools for recording and editing, tools for mixing, tools for creating RSS feeds, and a catch-all category I call podcasting applications.

- *Recording and editing tools* capture audio or video from one or more inputs, store the files to disk, and allow you to rearrange or delete portions of the recorded files.
- *Mixing tools* allow you to combine and mix any number of files together into a final single sound or video file.
- *Tools for creating RSS feeds* automatically create the XML code that allows listeners to subscribe to the podcast.
- *Podcasting application tools* have the ability to do any combination of the first three categories and more—they allow you to record, edit, and mix audio or video files as well as to automate the encoding and uploading process.

A number of applications combine the production and post-production tools into one package, and new products are hitting the market every day. See Appendixes One, Two, and Three for some of those that are currently popular.

How to Select the Right Software

Choosing the appropriate tools for your situation is key in making the development process as simple and as efficient as possible. Unless you have access to a staff of professional production and post-production resources, using software that falls into the podcasting application tools category is the most practical because using software from the other categories requires learning and combining multiple tools. Also, consider whether you will be using a PC or a Mac to create, edit, and distribute your podcast. As mentioned earlier, Macs come equipped to support podcast development, so you may already have all the software you need.

On the other hand, if your organization has the financial and personnel resources, you might consider using multiple tools for podcast development. This approach can give you output of higher quality, and the applications that have been developed for a single purpose, especially for recording audio, tend to be more robust. Applications designed to record, edit, mix, and publish simply cannot compete with audio recording software designed specifically to record. As mentioned earlier, the quality of the podcast depends to a significant degree on the quality of the sound that goes into the computer.

Another factor to think about is the format of the podcast you will be making. Is it a lecture? An interview or discussion with two or more people? Are you using voice-over or sound effects? Music? Video? How complicated will the video be? The software you select should allow you to carry out all the tasks needed for the specific format. (See Chapter Eight for details about podcast formats.)

Summary

Thus far, I've given you a look at some of the challenges that today's training organizations are facing. These challenges include supporting the increasing speed of business and finding training options that address the needs of today's workforce with its technologically savvy employees who have grown up with computers, cell phones, personal electronic devices, mobile audio players, and the Internet. These workers are accustomed to doing more than one thing at a time and need a constant flow of information and training just to keep up.

Podcasts can be an ideal option for addressing many of the issues of today's learning landscape. Podcasts make use of the electronic media that are an integral part of today's learners' world, and they present information in the snippets today's learners prefer.

A podcast is a digital audio program, a multimedia computer file that can be downloaded to a computer, an iPod, or another device, then played or replayed on demand. Updated content and new editions can be downloaded quickly and, in some cases, automatically. Podcasts are always available, portable, easy to control, automatic, and inexpensive.

Some pioneers in the training world have already adopted podcasts as part of their overall training solution, and I presented some criteria for deciding whether podcasting is the right choice for your organization—along with some of the legal issues to consider if you set up for podcasting. This chapter rounded out the background with a look at the hardware and software required to create a podcast.

In Part Two of this book, I outline more of the specific issues that training organizations face while implementing podcast solutions, and then explore the factors surrounding the development and distribution of training podcasts. I also discuss the podcast development process and explain how to identify and secure the resources required to create a podcast.

Part Two

DEVELOPING AND DISTRIBUTING TRAINING PODCASTS

5

OVERVIEW OF THE PODCAST DEVELOPMENT PROCESS

In this part of the book, you will learn the nuts and bolts of the podcasting process—how to develop and distribute a training podcast.

Whether meant for training or for any other purpose, podcasts are in fact productions more like movies, television shows, or recorded radio programs than like traditional training courses. Thus you go through similar stages to create them: *concept, pre-production, production, post-production,* and *distribution*. As shown in Table 5.1, each stage has its own series of tasks that must be completed for the process to go smoothly.

Some of the tasks involved in podcast development need to be carried out only once; others will be repeated for every podcast that you produce. For example, in the concept stage, you might establish the general approach and objectives for all your organization's instructional podcasts; once the tasks related to that decision have been completed, they will not need to be repeated for subsequent podcasts that are intended to meet the same requirements.

Similarly, some of the tasks accomplished during the pre-production stage only need to be accomplished for the first podcast in a series. Once you have designed an approach, or a format, you can use it again and again for subsequent podcasts, unless business requirements change or you decide to make adjustments in the format.

Table 5.1 Podcast Development Process

Development Stage	Tasks
Concept	Determine whether podcasting is a way to address a business issue, identify business requirements for podcasting, and set measurable targets for a single podcast or a series of podcasts.
Pre-production	Prepare the elements involved in production, including designing the approach or format, creating a storyboard and script, assembling resources, scheduling production activities, and rehearsing.
Production	Record or obtain the audio elements of the podcast, including music, voices, and sound effects, and label audio clips so they will be ready for editing.
Post-production	Edit the audio elements, add audio if needed, adjust the volume, and organize audio clips into the finished podcast.
Distribution	Publish the podcast—make it available to users by placing it on a Web site with a unique Web address.

Later in this chapter, I will discuss the five stages in more detail. First, however, here's a look at an instructional approach for developing training podcasts.

An Instructional Approach

To ensure that your podcast or series of podcasts successfully achieves the goal of delivering instruction, you must apply some type of instructional approach to the development process. One approach that works well is DMADDI, a Six-Sigma methodology that is used to identify business requirements and correctly measure the business value of training programs.

About Six Sigma and DMADDI

Six Sigma is a methodology that aligns core business processes with customer and business requirements, quantifying how good a job you are doing at meeting stakeholder expectations, and then applying tactics for ensuring that those expectations are met. Here's a good working definition of Six Sigma: *a customer-focused, data-driven, measurement-based strategy that allows organizations to meet customer requirements virtually every time*.

A major difference between Six Sigma and other quality programs, such as Total Quality Management (TQM), is that Six Sigma incorporates a control phase with ongoing checks designed to ensure that once improvements are achieved, they are not a one-time or temporary phenomenon, but maintained over the course of time. Six Sigma methodology gives those who use it a structured (yet flexible) process, a large and expanding toolset, a configuration to clarify roles and responsibilities, and a system of governance to ensure compliance.

DMADDI, a Six-Sigma methodology specifically geared for the development of training programs, comprises the six phases that form its acronym: Define, Measure, Analyze, Design, Develop, and Implement. Each phase focuses on specific questions: What are the business opportunities? What business targets do we need to meet? What needs to be learned? How should we teach it? Does our prototype match our design? Did the implementation meet both business and instructional requirements? At the end of each phase, a review allows the sponsor to make sure that the program is targeted to business requirements, call a halt to projects that have no chance of meeting business needs, and make adjustments on projects that have lost their way.

Here is an overview of the phases:

- Define phase question: What are the business opportunities?
  One of the first activities that takes place in Define is to assemble a business review team. This team, which is made up of project stakeholders, serves as a steering committee for the life cycle of the project. It validates the business requirements of the project. At the end of every project phase, its members meet to ensure that the project is on target to meet those requirements.

- Measure phase question: What targets do we need to meet?

  This phase is where the business review team identifies the business targets. When this phase is complete, the team conducts a review to validate that the specific business targets agree with the business case that was approved in Define.

- Analyze phase question: What needs to be learned?

  This question is answered by the project team that will be designing the training and producing the podcast or podcast series. At the end of this phase, the team presents its findings to the business review team, to ensure that the outcomes of Analyze complement what was agreed to in Define and Measure.

- Design phase question: How should we teach it?

  The work in this phase is also accomplished by the project team. This crucial phase is where the project team identifies the instructional techniques, delivery mechanisms, activities, and exercises. It is during this phase that a podcast would be identified as a primary or supplementary delivery mechanism. At its conclusion, the project team must again present its findings to the business review team for review.

- Develop phase question: Does our prototype match our Design?

  During this phase, the training program—in this case, the podcast—is created. At the review for this phase, the business review team ensures that the prototype podcast matches the Design.

- Implement phase question: Does it work?

  This is where the training program—the podcast—goes live. At the conclusion of this phase, the business review team validates that the program has met both the business and instructional requirements. Since there have been ongoing formal evaluations at the end of every phase, the outcome should be a foregone conclusion.

Figure 5.1 demonstrates how the film metaphor and the instructional design metaphor can work together.

Figure 5.1 Podcast Stages and DMADDI

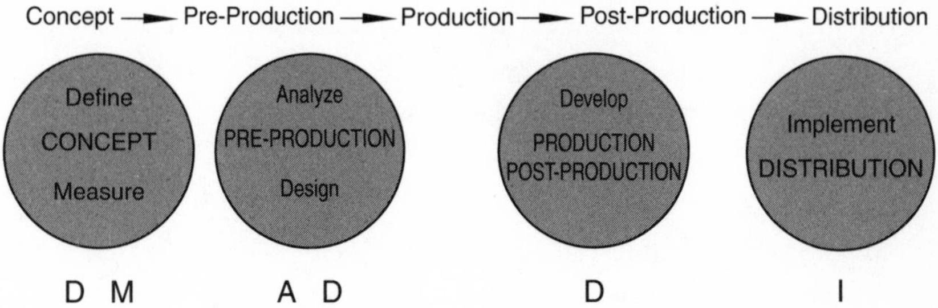

Concept ──► Pre-Production ──► Production ──► Post-Production ──► Distribution

Define CONCEPT Measure	Analyze PRE-PRODUCTION Design	Develop PRODUCTION POST-PRODUCTION	Implement DISTRIBUTION
D M	A D	D	I

DMADDI Project Organization

In addition to its tools, techniques, and methodologies, DMADDI provides a project organizational structure that promotes communication and accountability and helps break down organizational silos (see Figure 5.2). The project champion or sponsor is the person who requests the training program and thus sets the initial vision. The business review team sets the business requirements, determines the business targets, identifies what constitutes return on investment, and oversees the process to ensure that no decisions will compromise the program's ability to meet business requirements. The development team identifies the learning requirements and is responsible for ensuring that those targets are met. The project leader, or Black Belt, is the glue that ties all the stakeholders and processes together across the project life cycle.

For more information about DMADDI, read *Developing and Measuring Training the Six Sigma Way* (Pfeiffer, 2006).

Figure 5.2 DMADDI Project Organization

Project Champion (Sponsor)

Project Lead

Business Review Team · Design Team

The Five Stages of Developing a Podcast

The recommendation that you go through five formal stages for developing podcasts might give the impression that a lot of bureaucracy and time is associated with podcast development. This is not the case. Although all the stages are needed to ensure the success of a podcast, they can usually be completed quite quickly. As mentioned earlier, if the concept stage establishes an overall policy or strategy for developing and using podcasts, it will need to be carried out only once, and many of the tasks in the pre-production stage, in which the podcast design is developed, might also only need to be done once if all the podcasts you will be developing follow the same essential format.

Below are brief descriptions of each of the podcast development stages. The following chapters provide details about how to carry out each stage.

Define and Measure: The Concept Stage

The concept stage, which includes the define and measure phases of DMADDI, is the first and most important phase of podcast development. During this stage the business requirements for the podcast are identified, measurable targets are set, and a general agreement of what the podcast needs to cover is agreed to. It is in this stage that you make the determination about whether a single podcast or a series of podcasts is the right solution to a business issue that the organization is facing and establish the criteria by which the success of the podcast or the podcast series will be measured.

Once the concept stage has been successfully completed and validated, the project is considered "greenlit"—it's got the green light—and the process can move forward to the next stage, pre-production.

Chapter Six provides details about ways to carry out the concept stage.

Analyze and Define: The Pre-Production Stage

If the concept stage is the most important phase of podcast development, pre-production is a close second. Even with a simple project, many variables can improve or damage the quality of a podcast. The more thorough your planning in the pre-production stage, the more smoothly the production itself will go.

Pre-production, which encompasses both the Analyze and Design phases of DMADDI, is the process of preparing all the elements involved in a podcast and making sure that everything is in place. The tasks in this stage include identifying the learning objectives that need to be met or the topics to cover, deciding on a format, developing a storyboard, writing a script, assembling the resources you'll need, finding a cast, creating a schedule, and conducting any rehearsals that might be required.

During this stage, you might be focusing on a single podcast. If, however, you plan to produce a series of podcasts, or episodes, it is during this stage that you will make decisions and create a template that will guide the entire series.

Once the business review team validates pre-production, you will be ready to create the elements of the podcast.

Chapter Seven covers the pre-production stage in more detail.

Develop: The Production Stage

Like the Develop phase of DMADDI, the production stage of podcasting development is where the elements that make up the podcast are created. During production, the script that was approved in pre-production is recorded as audio or video clips and any accompanying graphics are prepared.

The time required for production will vary depending on the complexity of the podcast, the extent of the preparation that was invested during pre-production, and the experience of the producer. Obviously, the longer the podcast, the longer it will take to produce. Video also takes more time to produce than audio, since in addition to worrying about sound you must be concerned with lighting, costumes, setting, and movement. Video production also requires more hardware than sound production.

Many podcasters spend two to four times the length of their show just on production. The business review team does not need to review the output of production, but the design or development team should provide status updates.

Chapter Eight describes how production is accomplished using various podcasting tools and focuses on some of the general factors to consider during production. These factors exist whether the podcast is a simple production that takes only a few minutes or a more complex project that takes longer to produce.

Develop: The Post-Production Stage

Post-production, which is a continuation of the DMADDI Develop phase, is where all the components created in production are assembled and edited into a finished podcast, ready for distribution. The tasks in this stage include the processes needed to edit images and audio and to add any special effects. Typically, the post-production phase takes longer than the actual recording of the podcast—anywhere from four to ten times the amount of time budgeted for production might be required for post-production. As was the case with production, the business review team does not need to review the output of post-production, but should be given status updates.

Implement: The Distribution Stage

The distribution stage, the Implement phase of DMADDI, is where you publish the podcast—that is, put it on the Web, notify learners that it is available, and tell them how to access it.

To do that, you upload the finished podcast to a Web site and create a link, or address. Distributing your podcast can be very easy or moderately difficult, depending on whether you use an automated or manual process. This is the phase where the business review team is given an opportunity to listen to the completed podcast if members wish to do so.

Chapter Ten describes the options for distributing your podcast.

Summary

Podcasts are really productions that are more similar to movie, television, or recorded radio programs than to traditional training courses. Thus the five stages required to create training podcast—concept, pre-production, production, post-production, and distribution—are the same stages associated with movie production. Since the podcasts I'm describing here will be used as components of training, however, it's clear that they need some type of instructional approach to the development process. I recommend DMADDI, a Six-Sigma methodology that will help you identify business requirements and correctly measure the business value of training programs. The two approaches—movie-style production and DMADDI—work well together, and the activities mesh in each of the development stages. The coming chapters give you a closer look at each of these stages and walk you through the creation of a training podcast. Chapter Six explores the concept stage of podcast development, which is where the decision is made as to whether there will even be a podcast.

6

DEFINE AND MEASURE

The Concept Stage

The concept stage of podcasting is intended to answer the question, What are the business opportunities that the podcast must address? The first task in the concept stage is to assemble a business review team, which should be made up of people who have a stake in the project's success and the authority to make business decisions related to the project—but not those who will actually work on it. The business review team will then create a project charter, serve as a steering committee, and review progress at the end of each stage to ensure that the project is on target.

Once the business review team has established the general strategy for podcasting in your organization, it is generally not necessary to repeat the concept stage each time a new podcast episode is going to be created. The charter the team creates will establish policies for the organization's use of podcasting in support of solving the business problem.

Figure 6.1 identifies the major activities that take place during the concept stage.

Assembling a Business Review Team

Business review team members might include those involved in funding, managers whose employees form the audience for training, the director of an operational area, or product managers for products that training is being created for. They should all be as senior as possible—the more senior they are, the less likely it is that their decisions will be overturned.

Figure 6.1 The Concept Stage

Concept ──▶ Pre-Production ──▶ Production ──▶ Post-Production ──▶ Distribution
Assemble Business Review Team
Create Project Charter

The business review team's function is to validate that podcasting is in fact the correct strategy for addressing the business problems that must be solved via training, and then to ensure that all podcasts developed as a result actually solve those business problems.

Having a business review team set the strategy and validate the business requirements at the start of the process and then verify that the resulting podcasts satisfy those requirements across the life cycle of the project virtually eliminates *disconnects*, or misinterpretations of information. It also ensures that as the project progresses, any change of business circumstances is communicated as early as possible so that adjustments to the podcast can be made sooner rather than later. If you've never been involved in a project where something changed but the training department was never notified, so that you ended up delivering a solution that did not address the real business requirements in effect when you finished your work, you're among the lucky few.

To illustrate the way a business review team works, this chapter will follow the way one company made the decision to use podcasting as a way of training customers to use its software. For the background, see "ACME Technology Approaches Podcasting."

ACME Technology Approaches Podcasting

THE PROBLEM: Product managers at the ACME Technology Company (ATC) have traditionally looked to ATC's customer training department to develop and deliver training to the end users of the company's various software products. This training has traditionally been instructor-led.

ATC's business products were stable for many years, aimed primarily at a domestic market. The market has recently changed, however, and the organization now focuses on new or growth products that are being distributed quickly to a new global customer base. Unlike the old line, these new products undergo major system changes almost monthly. System users love what the products can do, but they have been asking for more, and more frequent, training so they can keep up with the changes and make the best use of the software.

In an effort to improve customer satisfaction, the CEO has mandated that product managers find a way of meeting the customers' requests. In response to the mandate, the manager of the newest growth product asks the customer training manager to develop "some more training" for his product.

After doing some research and consulting with her staff, the manager decides that podcast episodes that can be released every time a product is updated would be an effective way of delivering training to the company's widely dispersed customers. But podcasting as a training tool is a new concept for the company. She will need buy-in from key stakeholders on both the concept and the required outcomes.

To get the project started, the manager assigns one of her staff members as the project lead and asks him to assemble a business review team to create and validate the project charter.

Getting the right people involved is an important step. In the case of ATC, stakeholders include the product manager who wants "more training," his boss who wants improved customer satisfaction scores, the end user who wants frequent product updates, the developers who will be creating the update to the business application, and the customer trainers who are responsible for designing, developing, and delivering training.

It's important to make sure that no key stakeholders are left out of the process. A tool that can help ensure this is the Stakeholder Analysis Matrix. (See Exhibit 6.1 for an example.)

The project leader is responsible for completing the stakeholder analysis form, which is a matrix that helps identify a stakeholder's relationships to a project. This matrix can be used to help the project remain connected with people inside and outside the organization who can influence project success, identify strategies for involving stakeholders in the project, and keep people outside the team informed on the team's progress.

To complete the stakeholder analysis matrix, the project leader lists every stakeholder or potential stakeholder that he can think of and then answers some brief questions about the relationship of each stakeholder to the podcasting project.

Exhibit 6.1 Stakeholder Analysis Matrix

DMADDI Stakeholder Analysis											
	Relationship to Project					Involvement Strategy					
Stakeholder	Is affected by outcome	Can influence outcome	Has helpful expertise	Provides Resources	Has decision authority	Meet with regulary	Invite to meetings	Speak with informally	Copy on meeting minutes	Business Review Team	Development Team
Director Product Manager	X	X			X				X	X	
Product Manager	X	X	X		X	X		X	X	X	
Technical Lead			X				X	X	X		
Management Rep.			X						X		
Customer	X		X			X			X	X	
Instructional Designer			X			X			X		X
Training Manager		X			X				X	X	

Once the matrix is complete, the project sponsor or the most senior person in the organization should send out a letter to request that those individuals identified in the matrix as team members participate on the team. Please note that prior to this letter being sent out there must be communication between the sponsor and the various line managers who will be providing resources to get agreement and support. This letter should also introduce the team leader and point out that the project has the support of their line managers. Exhibit 6.2 shows the letter that the ATC podcasting project sponsor sent to potential business review team members.

Creating a Project Charter

Once the business review team has been assembled, its first job is to develop a project charter. This document serves as a compass to keep the project team headed in the right direction and ensure that the podcast accomplishes what it is intended to accomplish. For ATC, the purpose of the charter is to get agreement on podcasting as a solution to the training need as well as what business objectives the solution must address.

The DMADDI charter has six sections:

1. Business Case
2. Goal Statement
3. Opportunity Statement
4. Project Scope
5. Milestones
6. Team Members

Developing a good project charter is not an easy task and should not be taken lightly. The business case, opportunity

Exhibit 6.2 Participation Request Letter

ACME
222 Acme Street
Acme, NJ 55555

T: 800.555.1212
F: 800.222.1234

acme@acme.com

July 28th, 2007

George Reynolds
Executive Vice President
ACME Corp.
222 Acme Steet
Acme, NJ 55555

Dear Sarah,

Congratulations, because of your expertise in our ACME products, your management has selected you to participate on a team that is setting our corporate strategy for educating our customer base on ACME products. As a member of this high-profile team, you will help to identify the approach that our company will use to increase our market share and to increase our customer satisfaction scores.

The next communication that you will receive regarding this project will be from Paul Epps. Paul is a Six Sigma Black Belt and has been selected by the management team to be the team lead for this project.

Congratulations again, and I look forward to our shared success.

 Sincerely,

George Reynolds
Executive VP

statement, and goal statement each take on a different twist, depending on the perspective of the stakeholder. Thus, having a business review team that includes the appropriate stakeholders ensures that each component is looked at from diverse perspectives. If the stakeholders agree on the project success criteria at the beginning, the chances of having dissatisfied stakeholders at the end are much reduced.

Once developed, a project charter should not be fixed in stone. The charter is a living document. and as more information is uncovered in later phases of the project, updates should be made.

Exhibit 6.3 shows the project charter that the stakeholders developed for the ATC podcasting project.

Components of a Project Charter

The components of this charter are worth a closer look.

Component: A business case that describes the benefit for undertaking the project. The business case should provide a broad definition of the issues assigned to the team and address the following questions:

- Does the project align with other business initiatives?
- What is the focus for the team?
- What impacts will the project have on other business units and employees?
- What benefits will be derived from this project?

As you can see from the ACME 360 Project Charter, the project is aligned with a company goal of retaining revenue. The team's focus is to ensure that the monthly training is provided on new products until the products become stable. The impact of failure is a loss of $13 million, and the benefit is maintaining the revenue.

Component: A goal statement that defines the objective of the project in measurable terms. The goal statement should be a one- or two-sentence description of the problem that the project will address. The goal statement addresses these types of questions:

Exhibit 6.3 ACME 360 Project Charter

Team Charter

| D | M | A | D | I |

| Project : 1234 | Project Name: ACME 360 Podcast |

Business Case: New business product offering has increased the company's customer base by 28%. This increase represents 26 million dollars in revenue annually. Customers who are dispersed globally have indicated that they would like at least monthly training sessions on the new products until they become stable. According to survey results, failure to provide this training will likely result in 13 million dollars of lost revenue because customers will use rival systems. Changes to the new products are occurring several times per week. Because of the frequency of product updates, it has been agreed that communication and demonstrations of the feature changes will be communicated to customers via a podcast series, which must begin no later than 2/20.

Opportunity Statement: The company has the opportunity to retain 13 million dollars in revenue that it will lose if the training solution is not provided.

Goal Statement: The business review team will ensure that a podcast series has been implemented by 2/20. Successful oversight will ensure that 13 million dollars in revenue is not lost.

Project Scope:

Process: Ensure business requirements are met
Start Point: Project begins
End Point: Podcast series initiated

Milestones

Task/Phase	Start Date	End Date	Actual End
Complete Define	1/13	1/15	
Complete Measure	1/15	1/17	
Complete Analyze	1/17	1/19	
Complete Design	1/19	1/22	
Complete Develop	1/25	2/7	
Complete Implement	2/7	2/8	

Team Members

Champion/Sponsor:	CEO
Process Owner:	Dir. Product Mgt
Black Belt:	Project Leader
Core Member:	Product Mgr.
Core Member:	Customer
Core Member:	Training Mgr.
Core Member:	

- What is the team seeking to accomplish?
- How will success be measured?
- What specific parameters will be measured?
- What are the tangible hard results?
- What are the intangible soft results?

As you can see from the ACME 360 Project Charter, the goal of the business review team is to ensure that the podcast solution is implemented by February 20th.

Component: An opportunity statement that describes why the project is being undertaken. The opportunity statement answers these questions:

- What is wrong or not working?
- When and where do the problems occur?
- How extensive are the problems?
- What is the impact on our customers, business, or employees?

It's pretty clear that the opportunity for ACME 360 is revenue retention.

Component: A project scope that defines the boundaries of the project. The project scope identifies the start and end points of the project:

- What is outside the team's boundaries?
- What parts of the business are included?
- What parts of the business are not included?

Component: Milestones, the high-level deliverables, with tentative deadlines. The milestones section of the charter gives some basic time lines to indicate when important phases of the project must be completed or when important deliverables are due.

Component: Team members—everyone on the team identified by role. The Team Members section of the charter simply identifies each member of the team and generally describes his or her role.

Validating the Charter

Once the team has developed the charter, they need to validate it to ensure its effectiveness. Essentially what this means is that before considering the charter approved, the team members should individually and jointly take one more look at it to make sure it has captured exactly what the team is attempting to achieve. One methodology for charter evaluation is SMART. SMART is an acronym:

Specific: Does it represent a real business problem?

Measurable: Are we able to measure the problem, establish a baseline, and set targets?

Attainable: Is the goal achievable? Is the project completion date realistic?

Relevant: Does it relate to a business objective?

Time-bound: Have we set a date for completion?

SMART is thus a checklist designed to ensure that the charter is effective and thorough. The team should review each of the sections of the charter to ensure that they meet the SMART criteria.

The sample charter in Exhibit 6.3 is a good example of a DMADDI charter that contains all of the required components. The business case is linked to a corporate initiative to retain the

$13 million in revenue that the company is in jeopardy of losing. The answer will be to provide a podcast series that will address customer requests for more frequent training. The opportunity statement points out the pain or consequences associated with the problem in quantifiable terms by indicating that the company would lose $13 million if the solution were not provided. The goal statement clearly lays out the responsibility of the business review team, which is to ensure that the podcast solution is implemented by February 20th. The team members are identified, the scope of the team is clearly stated, and the project milestones are identified.

Agreement on the charter for the podcasting project signifies that the project—and thus the approach, which is the use of podcasting as a training solution to solve this business problem—can be considered greenlit and pre-production can begin.

Summary

During the concept stage of podcast development, the ACT team determined that podcasting would be a solution for a problem that the organization is facing. A business review team has been assembled. A charter documenting the business case, opportunity, goals, milestones, and team members has been established. This charter validated that a podcast series was the solution. The project can now move into its next stage—pre-production. In pre-production the details of the podcast content are hammered out. The design approach or format is determined, a script might be written, resources are secured, and production activities are scheduled. The next chapter turns to the activities that take place in pre-production.

7

ANALYZE AND DESIGN

The Pre-Production Stage

During the concept stage, the ACME business review team green-lit the concept of creating a series of podcasts to address a business problem, which was how to respond to customer requests for more and more frequent training on the company's new products. A series of podcasts is like a television show that has more than one episode. The series has an overall design, a template that specifies the elements that will be common to all podcasts in the series, and then a specific design, including specific content, for each individual episode.

Now that the concept of podcasting has been greenlit, the next very important stage, pre-production, can begin. A lot of work must be accomplished in pre-production. Generally, the major activities include the following:

- Choosing the specific topics to cover
- Agreeing on the podcast format (or the format for a series)
- Blocking out the show—arranging all the elements in order
- Creating a storyboard—a screen-by-screen description of what users will see and hear during the podcast
- If necessary, writing the script that details every minute of the podcast, including the words that any narrator or the cast members will say
- Obtaining the necessary resources, such as hardware and software; a cast, set, and props; the music, and the graphics

- Creating a production schedule
- Holding rehearsals (if needed)

Figure 7.1 shows the major activities that must be accomplished during the pre-production stage.

The more thoroughly this stage is completed, the more smoothly the subsequent stages will go, and the more likely the podcast series is to achieve its objectives and also the more likely the individual podcasts are to achieve theirs. We will continue to assume that the DMADDI instructional approach is being fused with the podcast development process, and thus while the business review team will be updated at its conclusion, the work in this stage is done by the development team.

Choose Topics

The first task that should be accomplished in pre-production is to get agreement on the topics that the podcast or podcast series will cover. As with any training program, this activity is often one of the most challenging. It is not unusual for stakeholders to disagree about what topics need to be covered in a training program. Add to that a review and approval process that relies on a chain of individuals who must sign off, and it is not uncommon for this task to take longer than all the other stages combined.

Because podcasts best support short programs with timely information that needs frequent updating, however, it is important to reduce the time needed to approve the topics. One way to accomplish that is to gather all the right people in one room at the same time and get their agreement as part of a collaborative process. Having everyone who has input into the learning topics together at the same time eliminates content being passed from person to person without the context or the rationale that went into determining that the topic should be covered.

Figure 7.1 Podcasting Pre-Production Stage

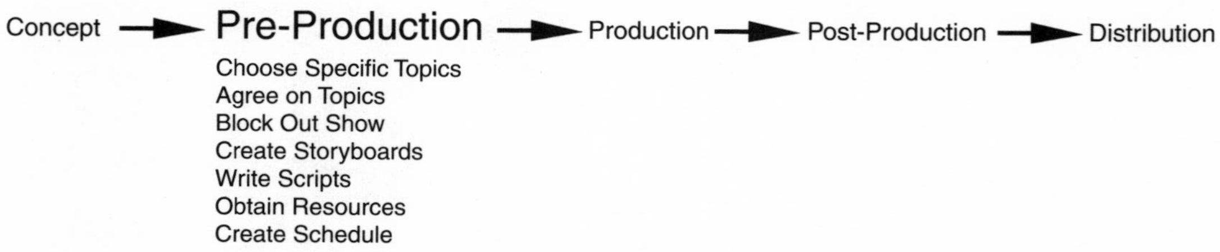

Concept → **Pre-Production** → Production → Post-Production → Distribution

Choose Specific Topics
Agree on Topics
Block Out Show
Create Storyboards
Write Scripts
Obtain Resources
Create Schedule

Who the right people are will depend on your organization and your organization's culture. One way of identifying them is to use the stakeholder analysis form discussed in Chapter Six.

This process can be facilitated by using a tool that encourages collaboration. One such tool is the affinity diagram, a brainstorming tool that is included in the Six Sigma tool kit. Figure 7.2 shows an example.

Here are the steps for completing an affinity diagram:

1. Once the group is assembled, the team leader helps participants brainstorm all the topics they think might need to be covered in the podcast or podcast series. The group members can write the topics on index cards or Post-it® Notes and then put them up on a board, or the team leader can ask people to call out possible topics and have a

Figure 7.2 Sample Affinity Diagram

Technical	End User	Mgt.
Functions	Help	Time Const.
Time Const.	News	News
Help	Time Const.	Help

Industry
News
New Funct.
Time Const.

volunteer write them on cards, Post-it® Notes, or a flip-chart page.

2. Once the participants have exhausted their input to the idea-generation process, the group can organize the topics into what appear to be logical groupings.

3. After all the topics are in the appropriate groups, the team can then eliminate any topics that on second thought do not belong.

4. When the team has agreed on the final list of topics and their groupings, the only remaining task is for the instructional designer to reword the topics so that they flow well instructionally.

We know that the ACME Technology Company deploys business systems software. ACT is currently putting an emphasis on new or growth products that undergo major system changes almost monthly. The product area has received low customer satisfaction scores in the area of training with customers, who say they want frequent training on the products.

We can also deduce from the scenario that the customer base for these products is segmented into end users of the system, technicians who must integrate these systems into their current infrastructure, management personnel, and industry experts. Each of these customer segments has a different agenda and a need for different information about the ACT product.

Although people in each segment are interested in how the changes or updates to the product will affect their daily interaction with the system, the segments use the system differently. End users are interested in information about how changes will affect the keystrokes that they use, the fields that they see, and the things the system helps them do, while the technicians are interested in changes that will affect the interoperability of the product with their systems. Their concerns involve what they

need to do to be able to support system upgrades and trou-
bleshoot technical issues. Management might be interested in
how upgrades or enhancements to the product might affect their
workflow or the number of personnel they need to allocate to
using the system. Industry experts might be interested in understanding how changes to the software product affect their
industry as a whole.

These and other factors influence what topics are discussed.
They are also drivers in determining the answer to questions
associated with the format of the podcast series, such as how
long each podcast should be, what elements it should contain,
and whether the main speaker should be alone or have a co-host,
as in the many radio or television shows that have two hosts.

For the ACME 360 podcast series, the team initially decides
that, since this is their first attempt at podcasting, they will identify only the topics that need to be addressed in the first podcast
in the series. The team also agrees to use affinity to get agreement
on the topics.

Each team member writes a list of topics on Post-it® Notes. All
of the notes are then placed on a whiteboard. The team eliminates
duplicates and rewords topics that sound similar. Finally, they
organize the topics into groups that seem logical.

The ACME development team came up with topics that fit
into four logical groups: the end-user view, the technical view,
the management view, and the industry expert view. Here is an
example of what the final topic lists might look like.

The End-User View

- Industry news
- New functionality
- New time constraints
- How to get help

The Technical View

- Industry news
- New functionality
- New time constraints
- How to get help

The Management View

- Industry news
- New functionality
- New time constraints
- How to get help

The Industry Expert View

- Industry news
- New functionality
- New time constraints
- How to get help

After further discussion, the team identifies that the logical groupings of information will remain the same for all subsequent podcast episodes and agrees that even though the specific topics might change, the groupings for each of the podcasts in the series should be consistent.

Choose a Podcast Format

Once the team has agreed on the topics that the podcast or podcast series will cover, the next task is to choose a format—a structure for each podcast in the series. Choosing a format means identifying the common elements that will shape each episode.

The format is the design that shows how the topics will be addressed. To develop the format, you will answer these kinds of questions:

- Will the podcast (or series) be audio only or will it include video?
- Will there be a host and co-host for the podcast?
- Will the information be presented lecture-style or will it be a dramatization?
- How long will the podcasts be?
- Will the podcasts include music? What kind of music? When and how will music be used?
- If you are using video, what kind of graphics will the podcasts include? Will you use animation?

This task is where instructional designers have the opportunity to get a little more creative than they might in traditional e-learning courses. A carefully considered format not only engages the audience, but it can reduce the time it takes to create each podcast. The more decisions that are made early in the process, the fewer changes that will occur later.

Design Factors

You need to consider a number of things when choosing a podcast format. Here are some guidelines.

Audience. Considering the profile of the audience should be nothing new to instructional designers. The same issues or concerns that affect the design of instruction in a typical training course should also be considered when determining the format for a podcast. For example, if the audience is nontechnical, you will need to present technical concepts in everyday language.

The answer to the question about podcast length also depends on the needs of the audience. A podcast can be five minutes long or run for more than an hour. To decide on the appropriate length, ask yourself, How and when will people listen to or view this podcast? They will probably not be at their desks. They might be commuting to or from work, or on their way to a customer appointment. They might be waiting for an airplane or in flight on their way to a conference or meeting. They might be taking a walk or working out at the gym. Ask yourself, considering the audience, what length is most appropriate?

How and when the audience will access the podcast might also help determine whether you use audio only or audio and video. Video requires more focus and concentration, so it might not be appropriate if the audience is likely to access the podcast in situations in which watching as well as listening would be difficult.

Industry. As with the audience, the industry that the podcast will address is also something that instructional designers are used to considering. The format of the podcast should be appropriate for the industry. Jokes about corporate scandals might not be appropriate for podcasts that target the financial services industry, for instance, and probably not for other industries as well.

Corporate Culture. The same concerns that affect the audience and the industry also apply to the culture of the company and should also be considered when creating a format for podcasts. If, for example, the podcasts that you are creating are for employees of a high-tech organization, a podcast with an extremely conservative theme might not be well received.

Host and Co-Host. Podcasts often benefit from having both a host and a co-host. Many people find a discussion between two or more individuals more interesting than anything a single narrator or lecturer can say. But additional hosts also increase the complication of producing a podcast, especially when you need to coordinate the schedules of several people across different time zones. The advantage of a single host is that the host is totally in control.

Music. Music is a great way to make the podcast more interesting. It adds variety, and it can be used to make transitions between segments, serving as a cue to the listener that the show is moving into something new or changing gears.

In addition to using music for transitions and to add variety, you can use music as an introduction. Introductory music raises the energy level and provides some momentum going into the show. If you are developing a podcast series, you can use the same introductory music for each show to establish a theme.

If the music you are using in a podcast is not royalty-free, you must obtain permission to use it. It's not legal to use copyrighted material in a podcast without permission. See Part One for more information about copyrights and the other legal issues relating to podcasts.

Putting Things Together

For the format of the ACME 360 Podcast Series, the instructional designer on the team should consider a number of factors. The audience for the podcast is segmented into end users of the system, technicians who must integrate these systems into their current infrastructure, management personnel, and industry experts. The cultures of the organizations whose employees will be accessing the podcast tend to be conservative. The designer also knows that the functions performed by the business systems change frequently.

Because the podcasts will need frequent updates, the designer decides that the format of the show should not contain video, which takes too long to create and edit. Since the topics are mostly informational, she also decides that the information will be presented mostly lecture-style but will use a host, co-host, and interviews to make the podcast more interesting. It will include screen shots of the application for the same reason. Because of the nature of the information, she also decides to limit the length of each podcast to no more than twenty minutes and use music to break up the different segments.

Block Out the Show

Once you've selected the format for the podcast, the next task is to block out the show. Like radio or television shows, podcasts consist of blocks called *elements*. Blocking out a show means identifying all the elements that the show will contain, arranging them in order, and specifying the exact time for each element.

Production elements are standardized elements that are generally the same in each episode. These elements include introductions, theme songs, and credits. Common types of production elements include content elements, or segments, plus transition elements, the "billboard," and the "teaser."

Content elements, also known as segments, are the real substance of the program. The content elements, which are where the information is presented, can include interviews, lectures, dramatizations, or even music. Great content segments engage, inform, entertain, or inspire the listener. In a newscast, for example, a content element might be the weatherman presenting the weather segment of the news.

Transition elements carry the listener from one content element to another. Transition elements tend to be short pieces of music, sound effects, or short speaking points that introduce the next segment.

The *billboard,* or rundown, is a short element that explains the contents of the podcast. In a newscast, the billboard element occurs at the beginning where someone says, "Our top stories tonight include. . . ."

The *teaser* is an element that excites the listener by offering a little information about what will appear later in the show or in another episode. In a newscast, a teaser typically occurs just before a commercial when the audience is asked to stay tuned for the next segment and then a preview of that segment appears. Teasers are also seen in television shows when at the end of an episode the audience is asked to "join us next week when our guests will be. . . ."

Here's a look at the format of our sample podcast series. Based on the knowledge developed to this point, the designer of the ACME podcast series might determine that the series be called "A 360-Degree View of the ACME Growth Product." This will allow each episode to contain information required from the perspective of each of the stakeholders. Each episode would begin with an introductory music jingle. This jingle should be repeated for every episode so listeners will identify the jingle with the podcast series. Each episode would also contain an intro by a host explaining what the episode accomplishes.

Five segments will follow the intro. In four of the segments representatives from each of the stakeholder groups will discuss how the newest updates would affect their industry segment. The fifth segment will be the host giving a summary of the episode.

Each segment will be separated by a musical transition element, and the podcast will begin and end with a musical jingle and accompanying vocals. To maintain audience interest, the content segments will be no longer than five minutes each and the intro and summary segments no longer than one minute each. The podcast will end with a closing jingle. Thus each episode of the "A 360-Degree View of the ACME Growth Product" podcast will be no longer than twenty-two minutes.

Table 7.1 shows how the ACME 360 podcast might be blocked out.

With the format of the podcast blocked out, the designer can now focus attention on gathering the resources required

Table 7.1 ACME 360 Podcast Blocking

Element	Duration
Intro music jingle	30 seconds
Show intro monologue	30 seconds
Transition jingle	5 seconds
End user view	3 minutes
Transition jingle	5 seconds
Technical view	3 minutes
Transition jingle	5 seconds
Management view	3 minutes
Transition jingle	5 seconds
Industry expert view	3 minutes
Transition jingle	5 seconds
Closing monologue	1 minute
Closing music jingle	1 minute

to create the podcast. She must schedule the resources that will represent the various customer segments, write and get approval of the script, obtain permission to use copyrighted music, and conduct practice sessions. Any software or hardware necessary to create the podcast should also be obtained during pre-production.

One tool that may be helpful in ensuring that as much as possible is completed during pre-production is a media requirements checklist. Figure 7.3 shows an example.

The media requirements checklist helps to identify all of the elements required for each segment of the podcast. It also contains a to-do section that provides space to map out the steps required to obtain any resources or media that are not yet on hand. Completing this form is simply a matter of aligning the segments to match the way that the podcast is blocked out and identifying any media elements required for each segment. The to-do section is used to identify the steps required to obtain the media—for example, to "record audio" or "get permission for use."

Figure 7.3 Media Requirements Checklist

Segment	Length	Elements Required	ID?	To Do
Musical Jingle	30s	Music Clip Audio	N N	Get agreement on jingle Record jingle Record intro audio
Host Intro	2m	Intro Clip	N	Record host intro
Musical Transition	15s	Transition Sound	Y	Insert transition sound
Customer Segment	4m	Industry Audio	N	
Musical Transition	15s	Transition Sound	Y	Insert transition sound
Industry Segment	4m	Industry Audio	N	
Musical Transition	15s	Transition Sound	Y	Insert transition sound
Technical Segment	4m	Technical Audio	N	Record technical audio
Musical Transition	15s	Transition Sound	Y	Insert transition sound
Mgt. Segment	4m	Mgt. Audio	N	Record mgt. audio
Musical Transition	15s	Transition Sound	Y	Insert transition sound
Host Summary	30s	Summary Audio	N	Record host summary
Musical Jingle	30s	Musical Clip Audio	N	Get agreement on jingle Record jingle Record summary audio

Develop a Storyboard

Once the show has been blocked out, you are ready to add additional detail and develop a *storyboard:* the screen-by-screen description of what people will hear (and see) during the podcast. You might not need a storyboard for podcasts that are only audio files—meaning that they contain no video or graphics—but if you do need a storyboard, you'll need to develop a new one for each podcast episode.

The storyboard becomes the guidebook for any director, artists, audio and video producers, programmers, and others who are involved with the production of the podcast. The storyboard provides a complete picture of the final podcast.

Storyboard Elements

Although storyboards do not all look exactly alike, every story-board should include these elements:

- Project information
- Screen label
- Descriptions of the audio—what the listener will hear
- Descriptions of the video clips and graphic images if any
- Description of any text that will appear on the screen
- Notes for the production staff

Project Information. The storyboard needs to include such information as the name of the podcast series (if applicable); the title of the specific podcast; the date, draft, or version number; and the script page number (if any).

Screen Label. The screen label indicates which screen of the program is being described. (Sometimes screens are called *events, scenes,* or *frames.*) Each screen label should be coded with the seg-ment number and a topic and topic number. Some practitioners put an extra zero at the end of the screen counter to leave room to fit additional screens into the script in the future. For example. if you needed to add a new screen in topic 6 between the existing screens 12 and 13, the revised script would reference the new screen as "06–0125." This labeling system can save a lot of time and energy later. Since artists name graphical images using these numerical screen labels as file names, this system avoids the need to renumber all the screens in the script whenever a new page is added.

Audio and Narration. The audio or narration descriptions on the storyboard describe what the listener will hear from moment to moment. Audio might be "narrator voice," "dramatic music," "buzzer," and so on.

Graphics. The storyboard indicates the graphics that are provided in the script as a verbal description of what should appear on screen. They help both the reviewer (the client or a subject-matter expert) and the artist who must create the final images to visualize what the designer has in mind. Descriptions might be specific, for example, "Show group of businesspeople around a conference table, gender-balanced and multiculturally diverse," or general, for example, "Computer on desk." General descriptions enable artists to apply their own creativity and resources. However, if the interpretation is too loose, the final graphic the artist creates may not match what the designer had in mind.

On-Screen Text Section. The script that describes the words to appear on the screen should also be included. Although this is generally not the case with podcasts, if the podcast were to have a screen shot of an application and on the screen there will be some accompanying text, this is where the text would be captured in the storyboard. In programs where audio narration is the primary instructional medium, the text is used to reinforce the audio. In these cases, the text is likely to appear as brief bulleted points or short statements.

Notes. The final section of the storyboard provides an area for any comments that do not fit easily into one of the other categories. This area allows the designer to communicate directly to an artist or programmer. These comments might include something like this: "The corporate culture is very young and enthusiastic. Let's make this opening screen reflect that. Feel free to get creative!"

How to Create a Storyboard

You have a choice of various ways to develop storyboards, including simply filling out a storyboard template that could be created by your organization or downloaded from many of the Web-based resources that are available. You could also use a software product such as Microsoft PowerPoint or Apple Computer's Keynote program to create your storyboard.

One advantage of using one of these software products to create the storyboard is that, if done correctly, the completed and approved storyboard can instantly be converted into a podcast. Applications such as ProfCast (www.profcast.com) allow users to convert PowerPoint or Keynote presentations into podcasts. This approach can save a tremendous amount of production time. Another advantage is that most trainers are used to working with these tools and can thus quickly enter the content (images, text, animations, and the like) into the slides. The script can then be added as speaker notes.

Develop the Script

A script may or may not be necessary for podcast development. If the audio or narration descriptions in the storyboard are extremely detailed in describing what the listener will hear from moment to moment, then there might not be a need to create a separate script. Similarly, if the podcast will not contain any video or graphics, a script may be sufficient to give enough detail on how the topics will be handled, and a storyboard is not necessarily required.

Scripts typically use verbal descriptions of onscreen graphical items, as opposed to storyboards, which use sketches or clip art to depict required art elements. Because of the time it takes to create even rough composite artwork, a scripting approach typically takes less time. The script provides the detail needed to produce the podcast. The level of detail will vary. If the podcast will consist mostly of interviewing subject-matter experts, simply listing the questions that the host will ask along with the wording for the opening monologue and teaser elements may be enough.

Any format that the developer is comfortable with will work for creating a script, as long as those who must read the script can understand the contents. One suggested approach is to align the speaking points with the segments of the podcast. Table 7.2 is an example of how part of a script for the ACME 360 podcast might look.

Assemble or Acquire Resources

Once you've finished the storyboard and the script, you are ready to assemble the resources required to produce the podcast, including voice or acting talent, software and hardware required, music, and locations for recording the podcast and shooting any video you are using. The media requirements checklist combined

Table 7.2 Sample Script

Element	Script
Intro Music Jingle	Play intro jingle
Intro Monologue	*Welcome to the ACME 360 View webcast for August 2007. My name is John Doe and today we will be interviewing end users, technicians, management, and industry leaders for the latest about ACME's derivative product, FUND Processing.*
Transition Jingle	Play transition jingle
The End User View	*I'm here with Sam Smith from ABC Brokerage firm. Sam . . .* • *What are the latest updates to FUND Processing?* • *How will these changes affect the end user of the system?* • *What are some of the benefits to the end user?*
Transition Jingle	Play transition jingle
The Technical View	*Our next guest is Jane Doe, the manager of information systems. Welcome, Jane.* • *Can you tell us about the latest technical updates to the FUND processing system?* • *What should those who are responsible for implementing the system in their companies be on the lookout for?*
Transition Jingle	Play transition jingle

with the blocked-out outline of the podcast should make you aware of most of the resources that you need to acquire for your podcast.

The ACME 360 podcast requires agreement on the intro jingle as well as the transition jingle. Here is the point at which a decision can be made either to use royalty-free music and acquire it at this point or to wait until production and create and record it there. Since the outline calls for interviews, the team must also get an agreement to participate from the host and cohost, a technical user of the system, a management user of the system, an industry user of the system, and an end user of the system.

Pre-Production To-Do List for Conducting Interviews

Contact for Permission
You must generally ask a person's permission for an interview. You might contact interviewees directly, or you might contact them indirectly, perhaps through a marketing or PR department.

Send Questions Beforehand
Many interviewees prefer that you send your questions ahead of time. When you send the questions, include specific information about the podcast.

Schedule Interviews in Advance
Determine when you want to air your episode, and schedule interviews at least three weeks before that date. That will give you time to conduct the interview and edit your material.

Give Your Interviewee First Listening Rights
It's a matter of etiquette to allow your interviewee the chance to listen to your edited audio file before it is broadcast. Interviewees may also work for companies whose attorneys must approve what they've said. However, keep in mind that it is *not* their job to tell you how the interview should be edited. They have the right

to approve their content, not the way you present it. Stay true to your message over your guest's suggestions.

Determine How You'll Record and Test

The location of your interviewee will largely determine how you'll record your podcast. You may want to use your hand-held digital recorder, your full podcast setup, or a conference call line to capture your guest's voice. Whatever the case, test your equipment and methodology before going live with your interviewee. Ask a friend or colleague to pretend to be your interviewee while recording and fix any tech problems. Repeat this process if necessary.

Depending on where interviewees are located, the customer-training department might also need to acquire some additional hardware. If that office is in another building (or city), for example, the phone patch that was discussed earlier might need to be acquired. A location for recording should also be determined. The best-case scenario would be if the customer-training department were to set up a dedicated recording studio.

Should You Use Professional Voice-Over Talent?

To create the most professional sound quality possible for a podcast, you might consider using professional voice-over talent. A voice-over is an unseen narrator, someone heard but not seen speaking in movies or television broadcasts, computer presentations, or Internet broadcasts. When you hear an announcer on a TV commercial, or a narrator on a documentary, the recording is called a *voice-over*. Professional voices add an additional layer of quality to any podcast.

Using professional talent to record parts of a podcast can also reduce the amount of time that it takes to record audio clips—professionals typically require fewer takes than amateurs do. The time saved on recording must, however, be balanced against the cost of professional talent. Prices vary widely, depending on where you are, the person's experience and reputation, and a number of other factors. At one end of the spectrum, a well-known celebrity could cost tens of thousands of dollars or more, while a local disk-jockey who does part-time voice-over work might be hired for far less. While preparing budgets, it might be a good idea to locate the talent you think would be appropriate for your project and find out what they charge.

Create a Schedule

Once you have identified the resources you'll need, your next step is to develop a production schedule. This schedule will organize the time, places, and people involved in creating the elements for the podcast. If you are using video, the production schedule should be organized based on locations, so that all video to be captured from a location can be shot on the same day if possible.

Remember that segments do not need to be shot or recorded in order. If the podcast contains a back-and-forth interaction, you can record all the dialogue separately and edit later so that it appears as though the individuals were in the same room at the same time speaking to each other. If you are using testimonials or interviews, you will want to record them first. Remember that everyone involved in the podcast must get a copy of the production schedule.

The more complicated your podcast, the more detailed your schedule needs to be, indicating specific times for each of the production activities. To create the schedule, you need to consider the following:

- How much time will be needed for each activity
- When specific people involved in the podcast are available
- When the locations for recording the podcast (and for shooting any video) are available
- When the equipment you need is available

Rehearsals

With the script written, the resources secured, and production dates scheduled, the next task that needs to be accomplished is rehearsal. The tendency among many podcasters is to "shoot from the hip" and "record on the fly." This approach tends to have consequences rather like those of doing a training course without first having a practice teaching session. It might go very well, but the lack of preparation might greatly diminish the quality of the product—and you can't tell which it'll be in advance.

It is always best to spend time rehearsing before any recording is done. If video is being used, rehearsal is essential. The ACME 360 podcast is based on interviews, so on the surface there might not seem to be an opportunity to practice or rehearse any of the material. This is not necessarily true. Time should be spent rehearsing the questions that will be asked. Even if the questions and responses will be recorded separately during production, practicing will reduce the number of takes required to get the recording right in production.

Summary

Pre-production is about making sure you have everything in place to create your podcast. It is where the team identifies the topics that the podcast needs to cover, agrees on a format for the podcast, develops a storyboard, writes a script, assembles the resources needed, finds a cast, creates a schedule, and conducts any rehearsals that are required. A tremendous number of tasks could be categorized as pre-production, and the natural reaction might be to leave some of these tasks for later in the podcast development process. It is best to ignore this tendency. If pre-production goes well, you will be less busy during production. Pre-production is geared toward organizing and planning everything as much as possible. The more time spent and the more tasks accomplished during pre-production, the smoother the rest of the process will go.

The next chapter explores the production phase of podcast development. This is where the components that make up the podcast are actually created.

8

THE PRODUCTION STAGE

In pre-production you develop the storyboard and the script for the podcast. If necessary, the people involved in the podcast rehearse the material. In production, you create the materials that make up the podcast. This is the stage where you record the audio elements, including voice, music, and sound effects, and create any graphics you will be using. You label the audio files so that you can find them easily during post-production, when you are ready to assemble them into the finished podcast. The time required to produce a podcast will greatly depend on the preparation and thought you invested during pre-production.

Figure 8.1 displays the major tasks that occur during production.

Using the Media Requirements Checklist

To keep the production process on track, it helps to have a to-do list of some kind, a checklist that shows you at a glance exactly what you need to accomplish. The Media Requirements Checklist described in Chapter Seven can serve that purpose.

Reviewing the Media Requirements Checklist developed during the ACME pre-production example gives us a list of to-do items for the media components for the podcast. (See Figure 7.3.) The checklist indicates that we must record the audio for each of the podcast segments, choose or create music for the opening and closing segments, and identify a sound for the segment transitions. This list of to-do items can be accomplished very easily

Figure 8.1 The Production Stage

Concept → Pre-Production → Production → Post-Production → Distribution

Record Audio
Create Graphics
Label Files

or with a little more difficulty, depending on which tools you use to create the podcast.

Setting Up the Production Environment

The first step in production for any podcast should be to set up the production environment to support the podcast that you are developing. This means putting together all the equipment needed to record or capture the elements that will make up the podcast and to store and manipulate them. (This equipment should have been identified and obtained during pre-production.)

Setting up the environment can be as simple as moving the laptop computer, microphone, and headphones into an empty office where you will be doing your recording or as complicated as building a small movie set so that you can capture video footage. How simple or complicated setting up the environment is will depend on your budget and the content of the podcast. The best-case scenario is that, once the concept of podcasting has been adopted by the organization, a dedicated full-time environment or podcast studio can be set up, to be used for all your episodes.

The ACME 360 podcast will not use video, so the environment needed is relatively simple. It needs a quiet location (preferably a soundproof room) with a telephone (for phone interviews); a computer, mixer, phone hybrid, headphones, and two or three unidirectional microphones; and all the various cables and connectors. Since setting up the equipment was covered earlier, I will not repeat it here.

Recording the Audio Elements

After the podcast environment is set up, the first production task is to record the audio elements for each podcast segment. The tools you use for recording might vary in the way they handle certain functions, but the concepts associated with audio recording remain the same. To record a quality podcast, you need to know a few things about recording audio, using a microphone, and making sure the levels of the audio are just right.

The best way to really understand how recording tools work and how they affect the sound is to record yourself, apply some of the effects, and then listen. That kind of practice will help you determine the optimal settings for your podcast.

Audio Concepts and Terms

Having a basic idea of some essential audio processing terms can help you produce quality sounds and ultimately a quality podcast. Here are some of the terms it is helpful to know:

Dynamics: Refers to the variations in magnitude in a sound. If a sound has many variations in volume, it is said to have a dynamic range.

Compression: Takes the loudest parts of audio and reduces their magnitude.

Limiting: An extreme version of compression. It keeps louder passages of a recording from exceeding set levels. Similar to compression in that it lowers the overall magnitude of a sound.

Gain: A fancy audio way of saying volume.

Expander: The opposite of a compressor and a useful tool for noise reduction. When a signal drops below a certain level, the expander automatically reduces it further.

Gate: A noise reduction tool. When too little sound is going into the system, the gate opens, allowing the sound to be recorded. When the sound level rises too high, the gate closes, preventing hissing sounds from getting into the recording.

Attack: A term used to describe the amount of time it takes an effect to engage once it has been triggered.

De-esser: a specific form of compression that reduces the harsh tones of human speech by increasing the amount of compression of certain frequencies.

Normalizer: Increases the volume of a track to its highest level possible before clipping occurs.

RMS normalizer: Applies a form of normalization that evens out the apparent loudness of a sound. It is also used during mastering, which is the process whereby all the tracks are combined into one recording.

Equilization: Allows for the altering of the overall emphasis of different frequency bands.

The Waveform

A waveform is a visual representation of the recorded audio. Once you understand the way the waveform works, you can "read" sound files. This is helpful when recording—and essential in post-production, where the podcast is edited.

The waveform, which tells you the sound level of the audio, is displayed in a window, vertically across a time line. Every audio tool has this display. If the audio recording tool can capture in stereo, you will see two waveforms, the top displaying the sound recorded on the left stereo channel and the bottom displaying the sound recorded on the right stereo channel.

The left side of the window generally displays numbers that decrease from 1.0 to .5 to 0 or from + to −. The number 0 on a waveform represents silence. The number 1.0 or a + sign means that the sound has been recorded as loudly as possible.

As you can see from the illustration in Figure 8.2, the dynamics of a voice create peaks and valleys in the waveform. In this illustration, from an application called GarageBand, notice that points of silence are depicted by a horizontal line at the 0.

Figure 8.2 Waveform with Silence

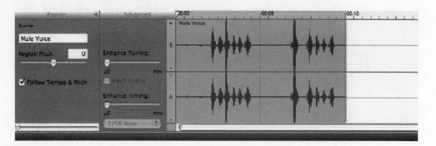

Recording Levels

The goal of a good recording is to get consistent levels of sound. A podcast using an interview with a subject-matter expert (SME) would not be effective if the moderator's voice was very low and the SME's voice came across as extremely loud. A consistent level allows listeners to hear the entire podcast without having to adjust the volume on their computers or audio players to compensate. One way to achieve consistent sound levels is to set a threshold for the sound levels of the podcast prior to recording, then have each of the speakers practice speaking in his or her natural voice. As they speak you can adjust the volume control to bring the sound to the appropriate level.

One common problem that you need to avoid is *clipping*. Clipping occurs when the recording level goes above 1.0 or the maximum level on the waveform. When that limit has been exceeded, too much sound is being pushed into the recording device and the output will contain a high, glass-cracking noise that cannot be edited out. Reaching that limit actually causes the audio portion at the top of the waveform to be lost (thus the term *clipping*), and once the sound is lost, it cannot be retrieved.

The best practice is to err on the side of recording at levels that are too low rather than too high. If the sound is recorded at lower levels, you have several ways to increase the volume of the recording. Keep in mind, however, that as you increase the volume of the sound, you also increase the volume of everything else, including the background noise.

The best solution for a good final output is to record with solid levels from the beginning. Try to find the balance of a level that is high enough to produce a strong signal without clipping. This can be accomplished by watching the waveform while recording and making sure that the waves remain at the appropriate levels.

Preparing to Record

Even though you might (and should) have rehearsed the speaking parts during pre-production, you should still do a few things before actually recording the podcast. You might compare this to a play in which the actors have rehearsed their parts thousands of times. Before the curtain goes up, they do a few last-minute checks to make sure they are prepared for that performance. In preparing to record themselves, speakers should make sure that they have the correct positioning, that they have developed the appropriate voice technique, and that they are speaking to one person at a time.

Positioning. To find the optimal distance from the microphone, speakers should recite a phrase or poem, or even a song, as they slowly move their heads and mouths from side to side, up and down, and back and forth to see how the different positions affect the sound. They should also adjust the microphone, chair, and sitting position (if the cast is sitting) so they can achieve a natural tone.

Developing a Voice Technique. When speaking into the microphone, the speakers do not need to speak too loudly. Check the levels on the waveform; if a speaker is yelling in order to be heard, turn up the volume on the headphones. The reverse is true if the speaker is speaking softly and the sound is coming across too loud in the headphones: simply turn the headphone volume down. If you have the resources, you might consider using a *sound engineer*, someone who will monitor the waveform for all the speakers and make sure that the levels stay consistent.

To develop a good vocal technique, it is important that the speaker be relaxed. While keeping the voice relaxed, however, it is also important that a certain level of energy is maintained so that listeners will remain engaged. Most voice-over artists record standing up. Recording in the standing position helps blood flow, breathing, and energy.

Talking to One Person at a Time. Talking as though they are speaking to a group tends to make speakers sound as if they are making a speech, and speeches have a tendency to sound fake. The goal of voice recorded for a podcast is to sound informal and intimate. Talking as though they are speaking to just one person makes the podcast sound more like a conversation.

One way of achieving the sound of talking to one person is to visualize a person you might want to deliver the message to, imagine that he or she is there, and begin talking as though you were speaking to him or her.

Recording a Podcast

Once you have set up your podcast environment and adjusted your sound levels, you are prepared to record your podcast. When the speakers have found the correct placement in relation to the microphone, gotten their voice technique on par, and have practiced speaking to one person at a time, you can begin recording.

As mentioned earlier, the process will be much the same no matter which tools you use. For this example, I assume use of the Audacity audio editor, which is available for Mac, Windows, or Linux, is free, and is a multi-track recorder.

Figure 8.3 shows the main recording window of the Audacity application.

Figure 8.3 Audacity Main Recording Screen

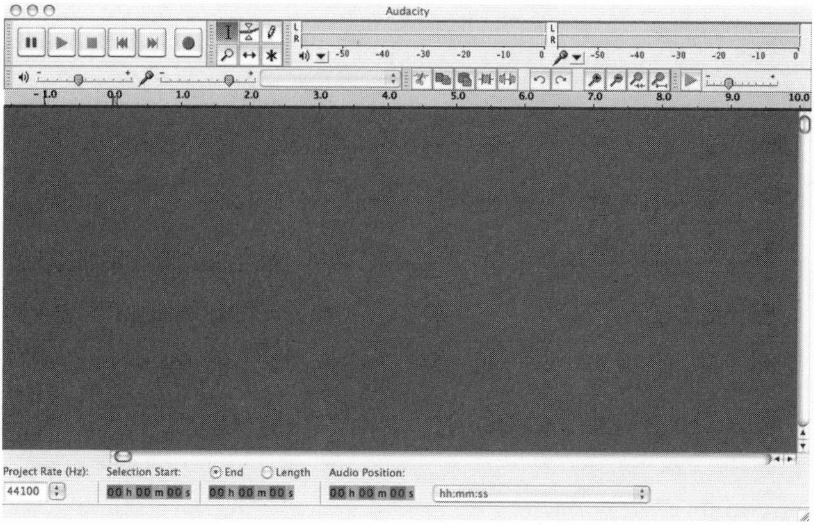

Setting Up the Software

First, you need to make sure that the software knows how to get the sound, at what rate the sound should be recorded, the format for most sound recording software (the default format is 16 bit, which means that the recording will be of CD quality), and where the file should be saved. This is accomplished in Audacity by doing the following:

1. Launch Audacity and create a new file.
2. Go to the Preferences window, click the I/O tab, and set the inputs to correspond with the appropriate recording settings. Figure 8.4 shows Audacity's Preferences window with the I/O tab selected.
3. Click on the Quality tab. Set the Default Sample Rate to 44.1kHz, and the Default Sample Format to 16 bit. These settings will ensure that the recording achieves CD quality without overtaxing the computer. Other software products

Figure 8.4 Audacity I/O Tab

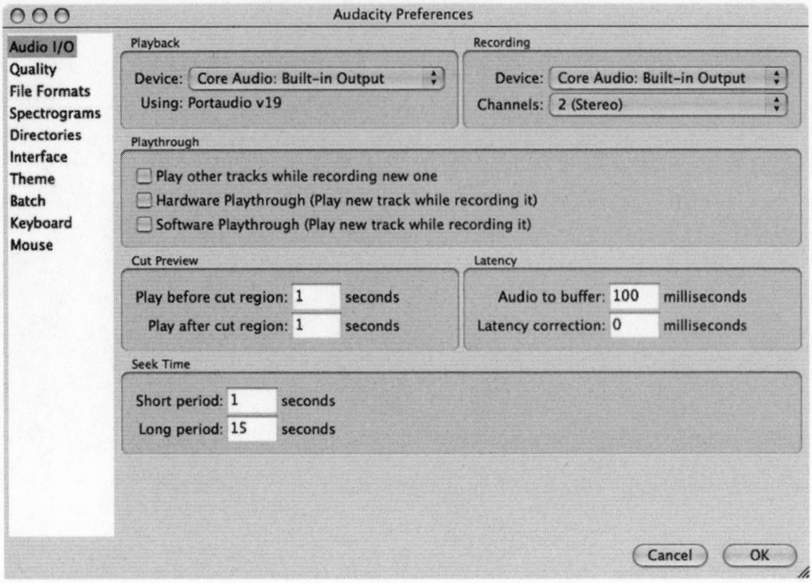

may give the option of recording in formats such as MP3, Apple Lossless, ACC, or WMA. Recording at 44.1khz rate and a 16 bit format produces larger file sizes than the other options but produces a better recording. Figure 8.5 shows Audacity's Quality tab.

4. Click on the File Formats tab and select WAV (if you are using Windows) or AIFF (if you are using a Mac). This will set your desired file format.

5. Click OK in the Preferences window to save any changes. Figure 8.6 shows Audacity's File Formats tab.

During pre-production, it was determined that the ACME podcast would contain comments from multiple sources. Thus, the best approach would be to use a multi-track recording tool and to put each of the different sound elements on a separate track. Organizing the sound elements this way during production

Figure 8.5 Audacity's Quality Tab

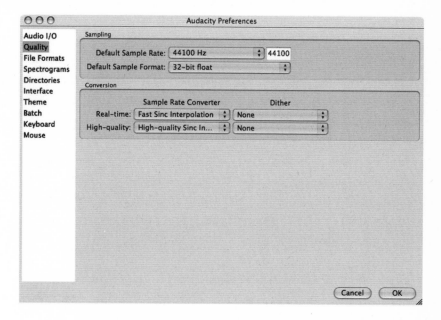

Figure 8.6 Audacity File Formats Tab

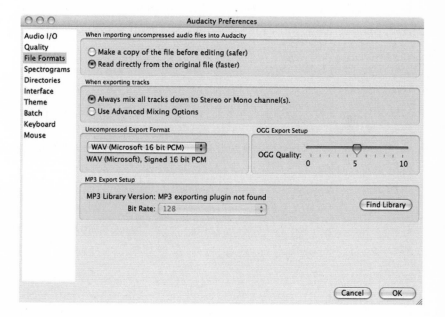

will save time in finding files that need to be edited in post-production.

A Note About Tracks

To fully understand how digital audio works, it helps to understand the concept of tracks. Imagine that you have two cassette recorders. On one you have recorded some popular music that contains no lyrics. On the other, you have recorded a colleague who is singing a melody. If you press play on both cassettes at the same time, you will hear what sounds like one song. The music is playing and your colleague is singing. If you turn down the volume on the cassette recorder that is playing the music, then your colleague's voice will dominate. If you turn down the volume on the cassette recorder that is playing your colleague's voice, then the music will dominate. If you turn either cassette off, then you will only hear the sound that is playing from the remaining cassette.

This is essentially how tracks work except that, rather than having separate cassette recorders, the digital audio recording and editing software allows each of the sound inputs to be captured or recorded in a different space or on a different track. Thus you can individually control the sound levels for each of the inputs. For example, you might capture the intro jingle on one track and the sound of the narrator speaking on a separate track. When you play both tracks at the same time it will sound as if you are listening to one sound file with a narrator speaking over some music. If you find that the music is too loud and dominating the narrator's voice, you can individually adjust the volume of the music track until there is balance. When the two tracks are combined or mastered, they then become one sound file.

Whatever multi-track tool is used will require configuration so that the appropriate number of tracks are available. Most tools have either an "add track" button or an "insert new" option as a menu item. Upon clicking the plus sign or choosing the new track option on the menu, you will probably be given the option of not only adding but also naming the new track.

Thus the next logical step in the process is to add the appropriate number of tracks and to name them so that each track corresponds with the audio that will appear on that track. Figure 8.7 shows GarageBand with tracks for each of the audio components that will be contained in the podcast. In the case of the

Figure 8.7 GarageBand with Tracks

ACME podcast, it should also include a track for the transition elements and one for the intro and exit music.

Recording Voices

With the software now configured, and the tracks set up to identify the various components of the podcast, it's time to begin recording.

When recording, it is good practice to test the distance from the microphone to the speaker to determine where the sound is the clearest. Headphones should be attached directly to the computer or audio interface for the best quality recording (sound from the computer's internal speakers will be picked up in the recording). If a mistake is made during recording, you can always do a second take and fix it when editing.

Production To-Do List for Interviews

You might use interviews in your podcasts. If so, it is important to be aware of some of the best practices associated with conducting interviews.

- Arrive early and prepare.

    Set up and test your equipment ahead of time so your interviewee won't get bored watching you fiddle with your computer and humming into microphones.

- Have a backup plan.

    Make sure to have a second method of interviewing so you won't inconvenience your guest if your equipment fails. The easiest way to do this is to use your full podcast recording setup as the primary unit, and to have a portable digital recorder as a backup. However, if you can afford it, it's better to have a second computer with a comparable podcasting setup. Consider recording with both methods anyway to allow greater flexibility and options while editing.

- Set parameters.

    Interviewees expect you to set the agenda for the interview. Explain how the interview will take place and establish your guidelines: "I know you've got twenty minutes for our interview. I have two quick questions for clarification before we begin recording. The interview will take about ten minutes, and then after I stop recording we can chat about who I should send the edited audio clip to for approval."

- Chat before the interview.

    This step will depend on the person you're interviewing, but the idea is to allow time to make your guest feel comfortable in front of the microphone. No matter how you're recording, you'll want interviewees to be quite close to the microphone for best sound quality. Let them get comfortable and then manipulate the microphone to its best position while chatting or setting parameters as described in the previous step.

- Ask some warm-up questions.

    Warm-up questions are designed to get your interviewee used to speaking into the microphone. These questions allow you to test sound levels before your interviewee answers the questions that are essential to capture for your interview. Keep the warm-up questions chatty. Use humor and try to get the interviewee to laugh. Loud noises like laughter will help you to tweak the levels so that they are appropriate when you begin the interview.

- Ask questions in a logical order.

    Ask questions in the order you sent them to your interviewee, or in a logical sequence that allows for flow of conversation. It's OK if you need to provide a segue, such as, "This is a bit of a tangent here, but. . . ." But try not to surprise your interviewees with material they weren't expecting. If they veer off topic, that's fine, because you can switch the order of their answers while editing.

- Be aware of time.

    Most podcasts are ten to fifteen minutes in length. That means an interview should only run about seven to twelve minutes to allow you time to introduce your show and insert your intro music, segue effects, and final thoughts. Depending on how many "ums" and "ahs" you want to edit out, you'll probably lose about thirty seconds to a minute of time for every ten minutes you record. So if guests get long-winded, rein them in or plan on a two-part podcast interview.

- If appropriate, send the link out to the interviewee.

    Your guests may want to link to your site so their Web site visitors can hear their interview. Make sure to provide two to three weeks' notice before you run your episode so your guests can announce it on their sites.

Another good practice when recording audio is to label the clips as you record them. By definition, a *clip* is a short segment of audio or video. Like our ACME 360 podcast, most podcasts contain many segments of audio that will need to be assembled during post-production. The best practice is to label the clips as they are being captured so you can find them easily later. This practice is not much different from naming files that you save on your computer. The names that you give each clip should make sense—otherwise, you might spend hours trying to find a file because you did not name it appropriately. After all, your desktop search engine isn't up to listening to the audio for you and telling you what's where.

With most recording tools, labeling clips as you capture them is an easy process. In most cases the speaker or sound engineer simply selects the clip that you would like to name and then types a name that corresponds to the clip. This tends to occur much in the way that you might name or rename a file on your computer. Ideally the name should correspond to the name that was created when the podcast was blocked out. For example, when blocking out the ACME podcast we identified that there would be a segment called "host intro." After we have captured the segment where the host recorded the introduction to the podcast, the clip should logically then be named "host intro." Figure 8.8 shows an example of two clips that have been named using Audacity.

A Note About Audio Recording Software

Regardless of the recording tool you use, you'll see onscreen control buttons that are designed to resemble the ones on a conventional tape recorder. Every tool has a play button, a record button, a pause button, rewind, fast forward, and a stop button. On some programs the play and pause button are the same.

To record the podcast, simply click the record button and begin. If speakers forget their lines or lose their place in the script while recording, simply click the pause button. To end the recording, click the stop button.

Figure 8.8 Audacity Clips

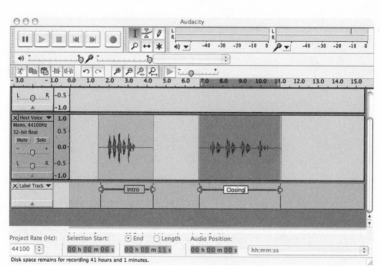

Music and Jingles

A glance at the media checklist for the ACME 360 podcast indicates that each podcast segment should be followed by a transition sound and that the podcast should begin and end with a musical jingle and accompanying narration.

Once the vocals have been recorded, it is time to add the musical transitions and jingles. Adding music can be handled in various ways depending on the software you are using. Some tools require that you import the audio from some other source such as a CD player or musical keyboard. Once the music exists or is opened in these types of podcasting software products, the music can then be edited and positioned or organized in the appropriate location. With tools that work this way, the music could also be purchased or obtained by downloading royalty-free music from the Internet.

You also have some other options for adding jingles and musical transitions to podcasts. GarageBand, the podcasting application from Apple Computer, comes with royalty-free music clips and jingles. (In fact, GarageBand has virtually all the resources required to create a podcast.) Podcasting applications that function like this are extremely convenient because they reduce copyright issues that you might face, and they make it simple to add jingles and transitions to your podcast.

Accessing these effects in programs like GarageBand is as simple as clicking on the view/hide loop browser icon, choosing the effects that you would like to use, and dragging them to the appropriate track. Figure 8.9 is an example of how this might look.

Video Podcasts

Taking a script or storyboard and turning it into a podcast that is more than just a talking head requires extensive planning. A successful video podcast combines many production elements—camera shots of various types, still images, music,

Figure 8.9 Jingles in GarageBand

transitions, titles, props, costumes, lighting, and sound effects. Used properly, these elements can aid in creating a compelling podcast. Organizing them requires additional planning and discussion during pre-production.

Tips for shooting video podcasts:

1. Keep the camera at eye-height, but also experiment with raising and lowering the camera to see the effect.

2. Keep actors who are not in the shot off-camera, positioned where they are supposed to be in the scene.

3. Take time to compose the shot. Objects should appear neither too high, too low, too close, nor too far away.

4. Consider the blocking of the scene. *Blocking* means how the actors move. When you edit your files you will find that it's most effective to edit on an action or some movement that lets you know exactly where you are in the filming process. Anything from a handshake to

putting a cup down on a table can serve as a blocking activity.

5. Always start filming ten seconds earlier than needed before the action point. Let the camera roll for ten seconds after the planned end of the shot.

6. Shoot the entire scene from one wide shot first.

7. Don't record over any of the takes. Even small parts of bad takes may be useful later on.

8. Show whatever is happening. If a character reaches for a box, shoot a separate close-up (a *cutaway*) of the box being picked up.

9. Keep a written record of shots in the order they are filmed.

10. Experiment with shooting some scenes at a slightly faster or slower speed.

Summary

The production stage is where the components that will make up the final podcast are actually developed. This includes recording any sound files (or video if used), and capturing or creating any music files that will be used. In this chapter I discussed various terms used in the process, explained how to set up editing software to record, best practices for interviewing, and how to label your sound clips so that they will be easy to find them during post-production.

At this point all the elements for your podcast should have been either acquired or created. The business review team does not need to review or look at any of this material, but its members should get a status report before you move on to post-production, where the podcast will be put together.

9

THE POST-PRODUCTION STAGE

All the components for the podcast have now been developed. The voice segments have been recorded, the opening and closing music has been captured or created, and the transition sounds are ready. Now it is time to edit and combine these components. In short, this is the post-production stage of the podcast development process.

Post-production usually takes longer than the actual recording of the podcast. The activities that take place during this stage typically include editing the audio, adding special effects, organizing the audio clips, and optimizing the podcast for distribution. Figure 9.1 shows the major activities that take place during post-production.

There is no one right way to edit a podcast. Some people approach post-production by recording live and simply hitting stop on their recording software package when they want to end a segment. This approach might be referred to as "editing as you record." Others spend hours working with editing software to fine-tune their podcast until it is perfect.

How much time you need to spend on the editing process depends on the complexity of the podcast and the requirements or standards for the finished product. Keep in mind that the podcast that you are producing will reflect on your organization. Of course, the more time spent editing a podcast, the more expensive it becomes and the longer it takes to get to market. If using the stop button to edit while recording the material is sufficient for your organization, then that should be your approach. But your

Figure 9.1 The Post-Production Stage

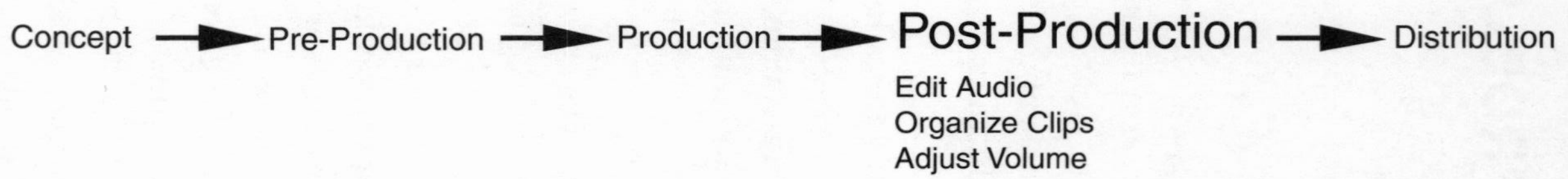

Concept → Pre-Production → Production → **Post-Production** → Distribution

Edit Audio
Organize Clips
Adjust Volume

finished podcast will be of a higher quality if you spend some time editing it after the segments have been produced.

Note: Today's podcast tools tend to be very inclusive, making it easy to combine the activities that take place in production with the activities that takes place during post-production. As tempting as this approach might be, I recommend avoiding it as it is apt to establish a circular development process—it can lure you into what seems like an endless cycle of updates and changes followed by additional updates and changes.

Editing Basics

During the editing process, you can correct any mistakes that were made during production. You can move, shorten, or remove elements of the various clips; rearrange segments to create a better flow or make points clearer; remove or correct unnecessary silences, mispronunciations, coughs, "ums," and other sounds that can make the podcast sound unprofessional, and change or add material.

Periods of silence in your recordings offer opportunities to improve the podcast by cutting material out or adding in new or different material. Accomplishing these tasks at silent points ensures that the final clip does not sound choppy or uneven. As long as the background noise in the podcast is consistent, cutting material out at moments of silence will produce edits that are virtually undetectable. If the voice tone and pace are consistent, entire chunks of the recording can be cut or rearranged without anyone noticing.

To edit the audio segments of your podcast, you will use the waveform that I described in Chapter Eight. The waveform tells you where you have long periods of silence, or where the sound is too loud or too soft. For example, a cough would show up on the waveform as a "spike" in the recording levels. During editing, you will remove any spikes as well as any unwanted periods of silence.

Editing the audio to delete unwanted silences or sounds essentially involves highlighting the portion of the waveform that you want to delete and then deleting it, the way you would highlight and delete unwanted words in a word processing program. The same concept applies when you want to replace a portion with something different.

The steps you'll follow to edit the audio will be almost identical, regardless of what audio editing software you use. So that you can listen to what you are about to delete before making the edit, most audio editing software packages allow you to play only the highlighted segment.

Eliminating Unwanted Silences and Sounds

The audio segments that you created during the production stage are likely to contain some unwanted periods of silence. Figure 9.2 shows a sample waveform that was captured with Audacity. The flat horizontal lines at the beginning and the end of the waveform indicate periods of silence at both the beginning and end of the sound clip, and the bands that cross the waveform from top to bottom indicate several spikes in the sound levels.

To clean up the unwanted periods of silence in this sound clip, you would simply highlight and delete those segments on the waveform, being careful not to delete anything you want to keep. Figure 9.3 shows a highlighted segment of the waveform before it is deleted. Deleting that segment will reduce the period of silence at the beginning of the clip.

As noted earlier, many audio editing tools will allow you to listen to just the area of the waveform that you have highlighted. It is important to do this before you make the final selection of what you would like to delete. You don't want to cut off too much of the silence because it could make the segment that is left sound choppy. (If you do happen to cut off too much of the silence, you can add silence later by adjusting the clips on the time line.) Figure 9.4 shows what the waveform will look like once the silence has been deleted.

Figure 9.2 Audacity Waveform

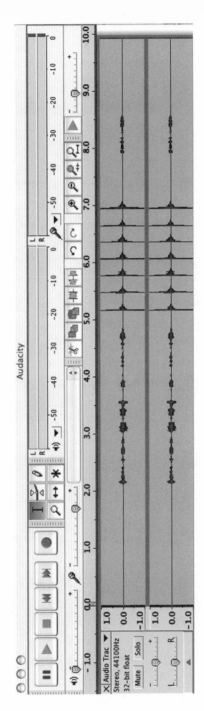

Figure 9.3 Highlighted Waveform

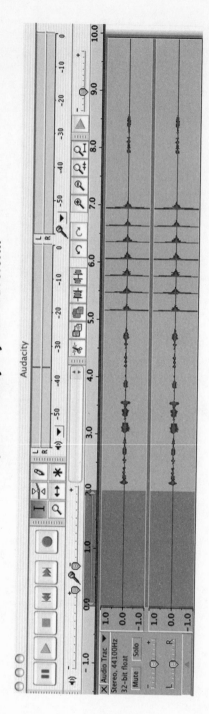

Figure 9.4 Silence Deleted

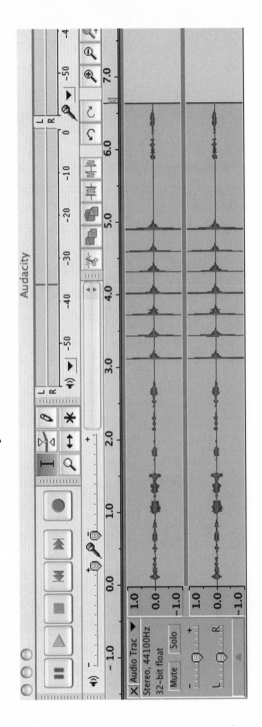

The same technique allows you to edit or remove unwanted spikes—bits of unwanted recorded voice, coughs, or other sounds that should not be in the finished podcast. The trick is to make sure that you have identified exactly what you want to cut out and make sure that that is all you cut.

Figure 9.5 shows a waveform in GarageBand.

That waveform shows what appears to be a voice speaking at a normal level, followed by some spikes in sound, followed by silence, followed by more normal voice. Listening to the track confirms that the spikes are in fact a series of coughs. To get rid of the coughs, you would do the following:

1. Highlight the spikes, as shown in Figure 9.6.

2. Press the play button and listen to make sure that you have captured everything that you want to cut out, and only that.

3. Once you are sure that you have selected the sounds you want to delete, use the edit button on the menu bar to delete them.

Figure 9.7 shows the waveform after the unwanted sounds have been deleted. Notice that the spikes are gone, and there is now a space between where the last normal sound ended and the next normal sound started. In GarageBand, this space indicates silence.

Adjusting the Silences

After you've edited out unwanted silences and spikes, you might need to go back and adjust the audio so that the recording doesn't sound choppy and so that the listener can absorb the information. People pause naturally when they speak, leaving moments of silence between words. Also, words that come too close together can be difficult to understand.

Figure 9.5 GarageBand Waveform

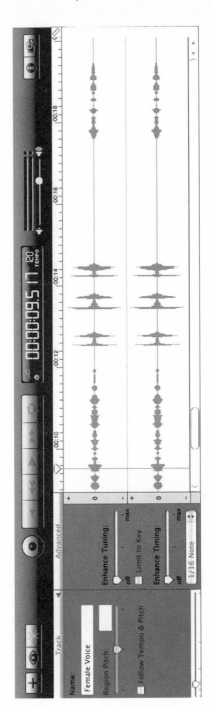

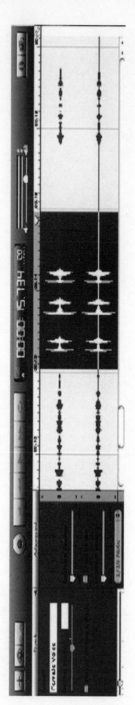

Figure 9.6 Coughs Highlighted

Figure 9.7 Coughs Deleted

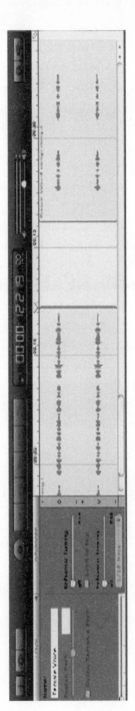

Adjusting the audio can be handled in different ways, depending on the audio editing tool that you are using. For example, with tools like Sound Studio 3 from Felt Tip Software (www.felttip.com) accomplishing this would require selecting the section of the waveform that you would like to move, cutting it out of the time line, placing the insertion point at the new location where you want the clip to appear, and pasting it there. With programs that function like Sound Studio, you can also increase the silence between two clips or even within a clip by placing your insertion point where you want the silence to be added and using whatever method the application allows for adding silence. Figure 9.8 shows silence being added using the Sound Studio 3 application.

Editing tools that function like Apple's GarageBand allow you to adjust the amount of silence by selecting clips and moving them closer together or further apart so as to reduce or increase the amount of silence between sounds. The best way to accomplish this is to listen to the edited clips. Experiment until you can determine how much silence to remove and how much to leave in, and then move the clips appropriately. Figure 9.9 shows a clip before it was moved in order to increase the silence, and Figure 9.10 shows it after it was moved.

Editing the Sound Levels

No matter how hard you might try to keep sound levels consistent while recording, you'll usually find that some clips are louder than others, so you will need to adjust them in post-production. All audio editing software has the ability to adjust sound levels. How this actually occurs depends on the software that you are using. Audacity accomplishes this task with an amplify feature. All you need to do is to select the clip whose volume you would like to adjust, then select the amplify option that (in version 1.3 of Audacity) is located under the "Effects" menu option. A dialogue box then opens with a lever that allows you to adjust the volume

Figure 9.8 Adding Silence

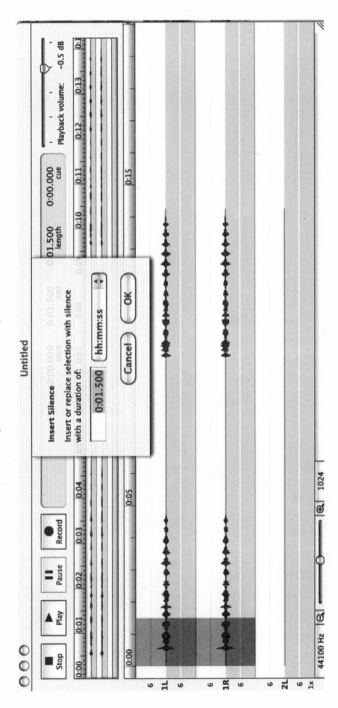

Figure 9.9 Clip Before Being Moved

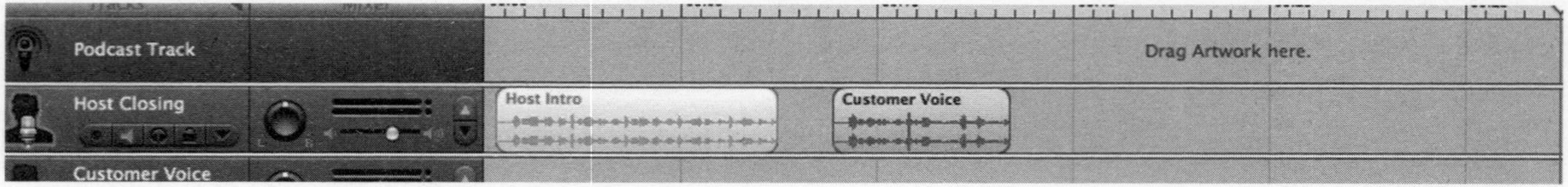

Figure 9.10 Clip After Being Moved

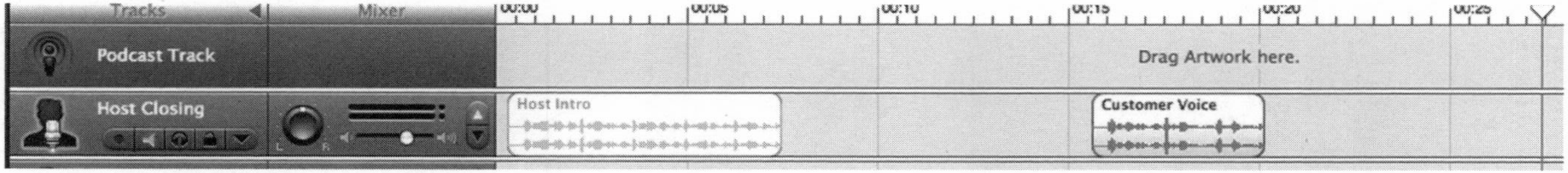

of the selected clip either up or down. Figure 9.11 shows the amplify dialogue feature of Audacity.

Organizing Clips

Once all the clips have been edited so that each contains exactly what you want and nothing else, the next step is to organize them so that the podcast makes sense. If you recorded the voices of each participant on a different track, many of these tracks will overlap on the time line, meaning that they will play at the same time.

More About Tracks

In Chapter Eight I spoke briefly about the concept of tracks. Now that we are in post-production, it makes sense to give a little more detail.

Recording and organizing content elements or clips on tracks offers many benefits. One is that when clips are organized this way, it is very easy to find things. As discussed in Chapter Eight, clips might not be recorded in order. Take our ACME 360 podcast, for example. We are going to assume that for whatever reason the industry expert was not available for a telephone interview but agreed to record the answers to the questions that we gave her in advance. She then recorded her answers, saved each answer as a different sound file, and e-mailed them to us. Each file therefore had an answer to one of the questions that we would have asked her in a telephone interview. She did not use any naming convention, just calling the answers file 1, file 2, file 3. and so on.

When we received the files, we simply used our audio editing software to import all the files onto a track named "Industry Expert," knowing that we would make adjustments during post-production.

Figure 9.11 The Amplify Feature of Audacity

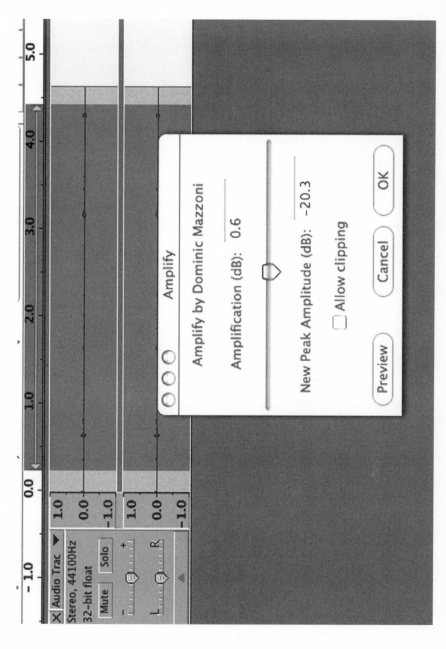

Now that we are in post-production, we look at our to-do list and remember that we need to listen to the files that were sent over by the industry expert to see what edits need to be done. Since all the clips are on the same track, we can locate them instantly.

Another example of how tracks make life simpler is in the event that wholesale changes need to be made to some component of a podcast. Imagine that you are producing a podcast that you initially decided would have some theme music playing in the background throughout the podcast. While listening to the podcast during post-production, you realize that theme music is a bad idea. If the theme music was recorded on a separate track, you could simply delete that track and all the other elements of the podcast would remain.

Tracks also expedite changes in the event of a major change in content—say that due to time constraints we wanted to delete the entire industry leader interview. Although we would still need to go to the narrator track and individually delete the clips that correspond to questions addressed to the industry person, all of the industry person's responses could be deleted by simply deleting the appropriate track.

As long as you have labeled the clips during production, organizing them should be an easy process, although the way you accomplish this task will depend on the audio editing tool that you use. Some tools, like Audacity and Sound Studio 3, accomplish this by letting you cut clips from their current location and then paste them where you want them to appear, just as you would do with a word processor. Programs like GarageBand handle organizing and rearranging clips slightly differently. With programs that work like this, you can simply select and "grab" the clip and move it to its new location the same way you could drag a file on your computer from one folder to another.

Figure 9.12 shows how the clips might look before you organize them on a multi-track program like GarageBand.

"Intro jingle" should appear on the time line before "host intro," and the "host intro" should be followed by "music transition one," and so on. Moving clips is simply a matter of dragging them to the desired destination on the timeline. Figure 9.13 shows what the newly arranged clips might look like.

Once the clips are arranged in the general area that you desire, the location and order can be refined by clicking the play button and listening for where you would like to make adjustments.

Deleting Unwanted Clips

While listening to the clips that were captured, you might determine that some sounds were inadvertently captured and you would like to delete them. This is accomplished by selecting the clips that you want to delete and pressing the delete key.

Adding Music

No matter how much planning took place during pre-production, once the podcast has reached the post-production stage, chances are that you will want to add something to spice it up a bit. Typically, post-production is where additional music or sound effects are added.

During the pre-production stage for our ACME training podcast, we determined that the production should include intro and closing jingles and transition music, so those clips were captured during production. Now that all the audio has been edited and organized, we might realize that adding some background music to one of the major voice sections will enhance the podcast. This can be accomplished easily with any multi-track audio recording application. It is simply a matter of locating the background music on your computer, or downloading the music you want to use,

Figure 9.12 Pre-Organized Clips in GarageBand

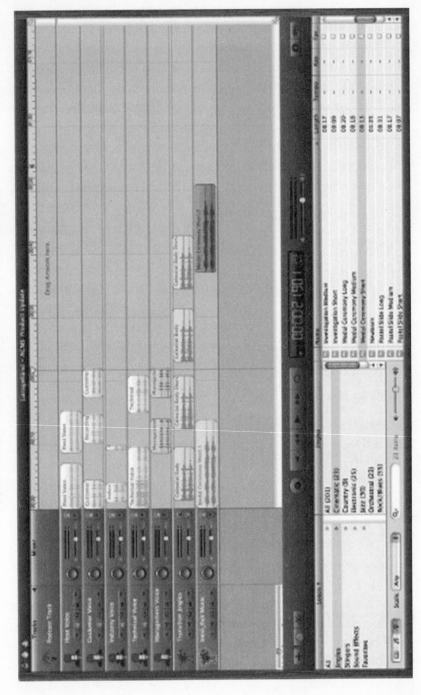

Figure 9.13 Newly Arranged Clips in GarageBand

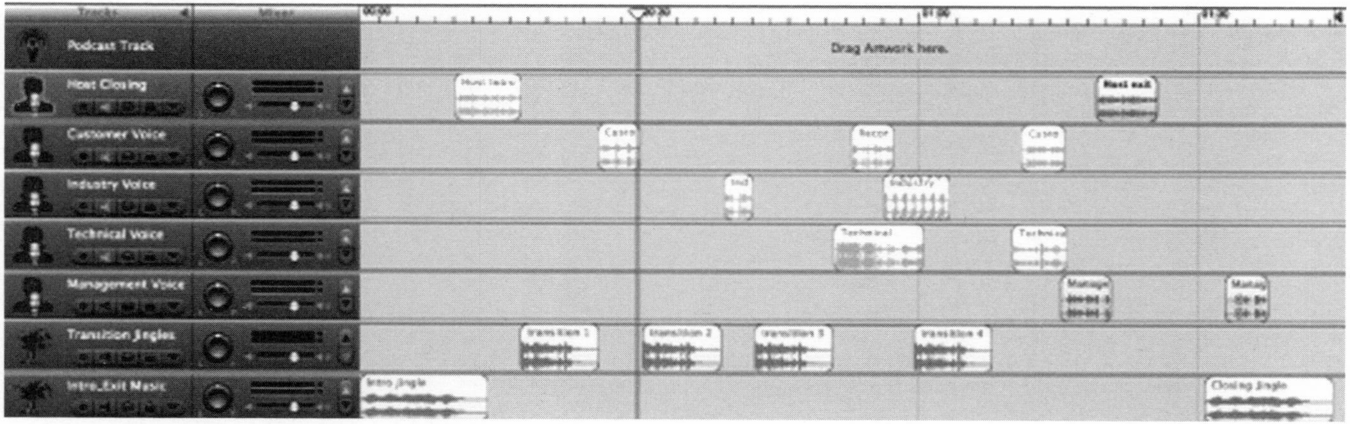

creating a new track, naming it, and importing the clip of the music onto the new track. You should then position the clip at the appropriate location on the timeline.

Fading Music Out

Once the additional music clip has been added, you may decide that you want it to gradually fade out so that the transition to the next segment of the podcast is smooth. Although a fade effect can be used on any audio clip, the technique tends to be used more frequently with music. Fading is created by leaving the volume at the beginning of the fade at 100 percent and gradually decreasing it to 0 percent. Virtually all audio editing software allows you to fade any audio clip out. Most audio editing tools handle this by having you highlight the section of music that you wish to fade out, then selecting some type of filter—usually "filter/fade out." The effect will immediately take place, providing a gradual, smooth fadeout.

Figure 9.14 is an example of what the waveform would look like in Sound Studio.

Optimizing the Podcast

The podcast is nearly finished. You have removed unwanted silence and unwanted sounds, set the volume of individual tracks, and deleted unwanted clips. The clips have been organized and some extra music has been added. The final step is to make sure that the audio sounds as good as it possibly can. This is accomplished through optimizing, or mastering.

Mastering is the process of preparing and transferring recorded audio to a medium that will be used in the production of copies, and the process by which the sound of the podcast is made as professional and as pleasing to the ear as possible. During mastering, you typically add filters that compress, expand, and normalize the sound. A number of filters can be applied to a podcast to improve the quality. I describe three of them here.

Figure 9.14 Fade Out in Sound Studio

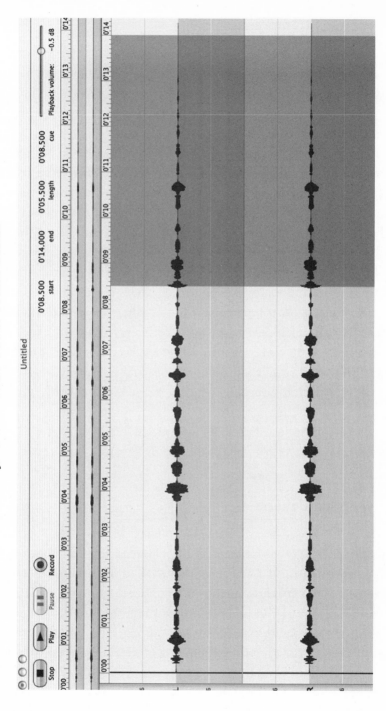

Dynamics Compressor

A dynamics compressor reduces differences in volume between quieter and louder sections of audio. It is applied to audio that goes above the threshold that you set. It smooths out the differences by turning the volume down by an amount determined by the compression ratio.

One way to describe the dynamics compressor is to imagine someone watching the sound meter on a stereo while the audio is playing and turning down the volume whenever the level goes above a certain threshold. This is what a compressor does. The compression ratio determines how far to turn down the volume when the level goes above the threshold, with larger ratios or differences between the louder and quieter sections of audio resulting in the volume being turned down more.

Compression is particularly useful when you are using music with a wide dynamic range, with both very quiet and very loud passages. Using compression, you can adjust the sound levels so that all the passages play at about the same volume. Compression is also used when sound levels vary because a speaker has moved closer to or farther from the microphone. Compression can compensate for these differences and produce a consistent level of audio.

Dynamics Expander

Just as a compressor reduces the differences in volume between louder and quieter sections of audio, an expander increases them. It works by turning down the volume when the volume level stays below some level that you set or the threshold level, and turning the volume back up when the level rises above the threshold. Imagine that someone has a hand on an input volume control. As the person on the microphone stops speaking, the person with the volume control turns the volume down lower so that the background noise is not heard. When the person with the microphone begins speaking again, the one with the control turns the volume back up. The expander accentuates the quiet and as a result alleviates the background noise, room noise, and even breathing sounds. When the person being recorded stops speaking, the expander automatically reduces the input level and does not increase it until the person begins speaking again.

Expanding is useful if you have a noisy recording and want to reduce the volume of the quieter passages so you don't notice the noise as much. It does have the side effect of changing the way sounds deteriorate, and during quieter parts of the audio, it can lower the levels so much that the sound cannot be heard.

Normalize

When the normalize filter is applied to a sound file, the filter scans the selected audio for peaks and adjusts the volume so that the peaks coincide with a target level that you specify. In other words, the volume is adjusted to the highest level possible before clipping occurs. The target level is shown in both decibels (dB) and percentage factor (%), with 0 dB being the maximum bandwidth of the file, and lower levels being negative decibel numbers. Figure 9.15 is an example of what the normalize filter looks like in Audacity.

The normalize filter can be applied in two ways, to individual tracks and to all tracks:

- *Normalize each track independently:* This option will treat each track separately when searching for and adjusting the peak levels. When multiple tracks are selected, this option will effectively bring each track to about the same volume relative to the others.

- *Normalize all tracks together:* This option will treat all tracks as a unit when searching for and adjusting the peak levels. When multiple tracks are selected, only the highest peak level of all tracks is considered. Each track is adjusted by the same amount so that the volume of each track relative to the others will stay the same.

Figure 9.15 Normalize Filter in Audacity

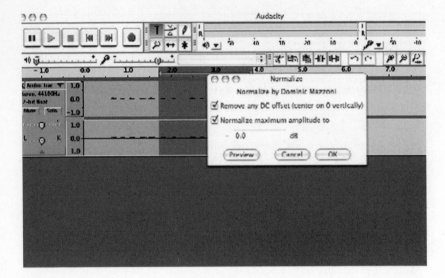

Final Review

Once post-production is complete, the business review team should have the opportunity to view the podcast before it is distributed to the learner community. If you have followed the DMADDI process correctly, this review will probably just be a rubber stamp because the production team has been updating the business review team throughout the entire process. The best practice is for the sign-off to take place as part of a tollgate review as prescribed by DMADDI.

More information about DMADDI can be found in *Developing and Measuring Training the Six Sigma Way* (Pfeiffer, 2006).

Summary

Post-production is the stage where the components of the podcast should be assembled, edited, organized, and optimized for delivery. Post-production is also the last opportunity that you will have to add any special effects or music to the podcast. The amount of time that post-production requires will depend largely on how good a job you did in pre-production. The next chapter will look at the final stage of podcast development—distributing the podcast to the target audience.

10

THE DISTRIBUTION STAGE

Congratulations, our ACME 360 podcast is just about ready to be published to its final location so that learners can have access to it.

To recap what has occurred in the process thus far, we have obtained agreement from our business stakeholders on the concept of a podcast. These stakeholders also participated in identifying some very specific goals for the program. We then got agreement from our stakeholders on the topics that the podcast needed to cover. We established a format for the show, blocked it out, and captured all the media required to put the show together. We then organized and edited each of the clips, and we optimized the entire podcast. The show is ready for distribution.

What this means is that we need to establish a place to store the podcast, and we need to create a Web link that people can use to find and download the file. Before I can talk about distributing or publishing a podcast so that learners can access it, however, I need to explain how a podcast finds its way to the learner's computer.

Downloading a podcast is a simple process that requires only three components: the podcast itself, the RSS feed, and a podcatcher. As noted earlier, a podcast is an MP3 file. The RSS feed is a piece of XML (not quite an acronym for *extensible markup language*) code that is stored on the Web as a raw text file, and a podcatcher is software that checks for new instances or new episodes of the podcast.

When the learner goes to a Web site that hosts the pod-cast and clicks on the subscribe button, the podcatcher soft-ware is programmed to automatically go to the location identified in the RSS feed to see if there is a new episode. If there is, the podcatcher downloads the file or episode to your computer. Figure 10.1 illustrates this process.

During the distribution stage, you will accomplish the two major tasks as shown in Figure 10.2: preparing the file for distri-bution and uploading the file to its final location.

Preparing the Podcast for Distribution

Truth be told, all the steps that took place during post-production can be considered part of preparing the podcast for distribution. There are, however, two more steps you need to take to prepare the podcast for distribution: converting the file to the MP3 format, and tagging the file so that people know where it came from.

Converting Files to the MP3 Format

Even with all the processing and filtering that have been done to the podcast thus far, the file will still be much too large for people

Figure 10.1 Podcast Process

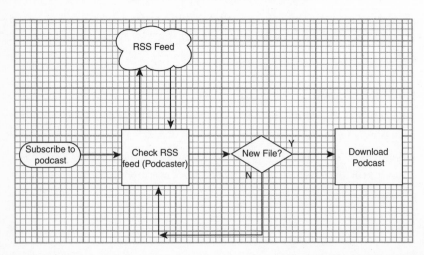

Figure 10.2 The Distribution Stage

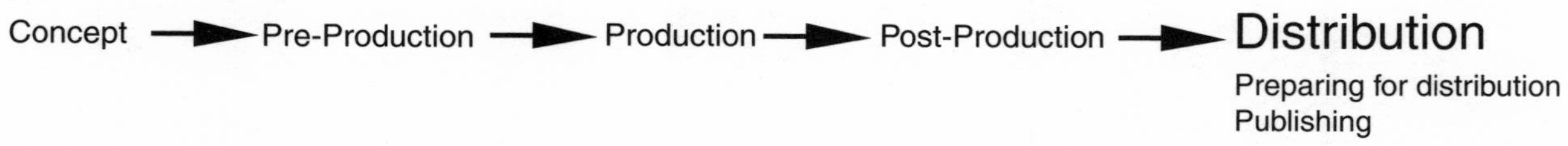

Concept ➤ Pre-Production ➤ Production ➤ Post-Production ➤ Distribution

Preparing for distribution
Publishing

to download (bring down from the Internet to their computers), and too big for you to upload (publish from your computer to the Internet) in a reasonable time. Compressing the file using the MPEG-1 Audio Layer 3 format (better known as the MP3 format) significantly reduces the size of the file.

Throwing out or eliminating bits of information from the sound file achieves this compression. The *codec* (that is, the program capable of performing encoding and decoding on a digital data stream or signal) used is designed to balance file size with quality. It accomplishes this by distinguishing between things that are important to maintain audio fidelity and intelligibility and those that are not. In short, the MP3 codec makes the file smaller by getting rid of bits of information in the file, and does it in a way that balances file size and the quality of the audio.

Regardless of the approach you use, compression causes sound quality to deteriorate. MP3 compression strikes a good balance between audio that is pleasing to the ear and a file size that is small enough so that it can be easily transferred. The MP3 codec accomplishes this with perceptual coding, a process that uses algorithms designed to encode and compress the audio signal while maintaining fidelity to the human ear.

Encoding Software

Many software packages do a great job of encoding or compressing files. The easiest to use are the software packages that allow you to export directly from the recording application to MP3. Most of the currently available podcast application packages, including Sound Studio and GarageBand, will do the encoding for you.

If the organization is not using an application that exports directly to MP3, a good starting point is to use either Apple iTunes or Audacity using the LAME encoder. LAME is an open-source MP3 encoder that is highly configurable and thus allows you to select very specific settings for how you want to go about the encoding process. Both iTunes and Audacity are currently free, easy to use, and available for both MAC and PC. A list of some popular encoding software is available in the appendixes.

Updating ID3 tags

When the ACME podcast is finally downloaded to the learners' computers, you want to make sure that it is easy for them to see where the file came from, who created it, and how to get more information about it. All this information is stored in the form of ID3 tags.

ID3 tags are chunks of data that media players can read, making information about each MP3 file or each training podcast easily available. Since these tags were originally designed to support music files, they generally ask for information such as name, artist, and album. Nevertheless, it is important for you to use these tags so that the learner knows the name of the training podcast, the individual or organization responsible for creating it, the URL, an e-mail address, and any other information, including artwork, that you would like associated with the training podcast.

Creating ID3 tags. Different programs create ID3 tags differently. The easiest ones to use are those that automate the process of creating the tags. Regardless of the application, creating ID3 tags is generally handled by selecting the podcast, choosing the option that the application uses to allow you to view information about the podcast, typing in the appropriate information, and then clicking the OK button. Figure 10.3 is an example of what this might look like in iTunes.

Adding Artwork. If it's appropriate, you might want to add album art to the ID3 tag. Album art is the image that represents your podcast. Whenever learners go to the Internet to download your podcast, this image will be there as a representation.

Figure 10.3 iTunes ID3 Info

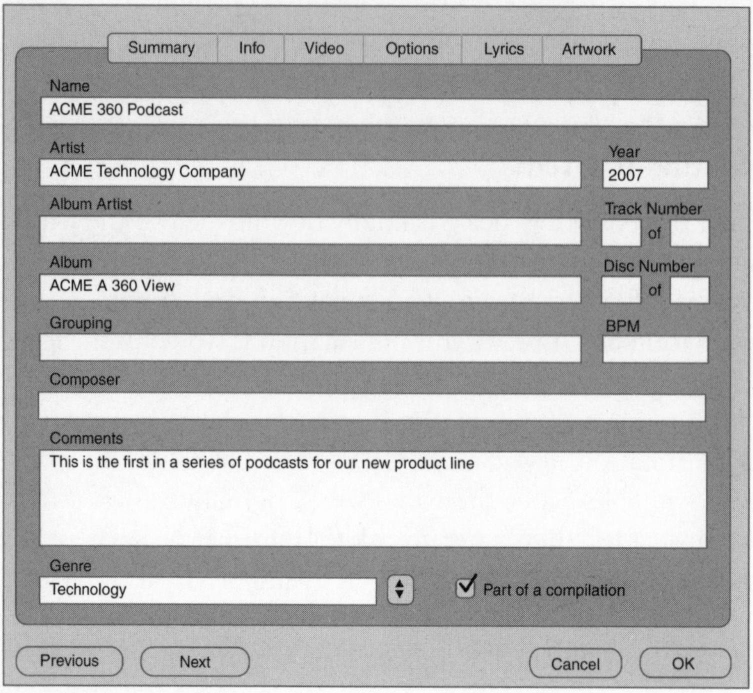

| Summary | Info | Video | Options | Lyrics | Artwork |

Name
ACME 360 Podcast

Artist
ACME Technology Company

Year
2007

Album Artist

Track Number
of

Album
ACME A 360 View

Disc Number
of

Grouping

BPM

Composer

Comments
This is the first in a series of podcasts for our new product line

Genre
Technology

☑ Part of a compilation

Previous   Next   Cancel   OK

Album art is a great way to add visual appeal to the show right in the file. Depending on how learners will be accessing the podcast, this might be the only visual representation they see. The album artwork can take up to a full screen, but renders more clearly if it is kept to a reasonable size. As was the case with ID3 tags, different programs handle this activity slightly differently, but essentially the steps are the same as with adding ID3 tags except that you would choose a tab or option that allows you to add artwork.

Uploading the podcast

Now that the ID3 tags and the album art have been added, the ACME 360 podcast is ready to be uploaded to its final location. How this occurs depends largely on where the podcast will reside.

Will the podcast be launched from a corporate intranet, or will it be accessed via the public Internet? This decision may well be an outgrowth of corporate policy, and you might not have a say. For the ACME 360 podcast, assume that the podcast will ultimately reside on the Internet since the content is targeted toward customers.

Regardless of the location to which you plan to publish the podcast, you need to make an important decision: whether to publish the podcast to an HTML site or to a blog site.

HTML Sites Versus Blog Sites

Generally, blogs are easy to update and require minimal knowledge of HTML. This factor alone can shape the decision, especially if your training organization has little IT support. Blogs require very little experience to set up and usually have an intuitive creation procedure.

HTML creation tools can be intimidating, especially to novices. HTML sites, however, have advantages because the design of the site is limited only by the imagination and skill of the designer. Table 10.1 gives a comparison of some of the issues between blog sites and HTML sites.

RSS Feeds

Unless you are using a podcast application that creates a Really Simple Syndication (RSS) feed for you, you'll need to know how to set up an RSS feed yourself.

RSS files are among the most widely used XML formats on the Web. They provide an open format for syndicating or allowing individuals to subscribe to all types of content, including podcasts. In short, an RSS feed is a page of raw code that is stored on the Internet to be read by podcatcher software on the learner's computer. Podcatchers use a Web feed to retrieve syndicated Web content like podcasts. When the content is published in a

Table 10.1 HTML and Blog Site Comparison

Issue	HTML Site	Blog Site
Price	High-end development tool; can be expensive.	Most blog software is free.
Layout	Great flexibility in creating page layouts. Tougher learning curve.	Little design required for new postings. Virtually no learning curve required to start.
Feedback	Not set up to accept feedback easily.	Most blogs are set up to welcome feedback or comments from listeners.
Feed creation	RSS feeds must be created separately.	Most blogs create an RSS feed that handles the podcast enclosure automatically.
Uploading	Most tools offer seamless uploading.	Tend to simply require the click of a button.

standard format, anybody anywhere in the world can subscribe to the feed and get the podcast automatically. If the feed is set up on a corporate intranet, individual employees can subscribe, but the podcast will not be accessible to the general public.

Setting up an RSS feed can be very easy or moderately difficult, depending on the approach used. That approach depends to a great extent on whether the organization will host the podcast on its own servers or use a hosted solution such as iTunes or iBlogger, as well as on the tools that were used to create the podcast. Regardless of the tools used, however, RSS files are made up of a channel, which has a title, link, description, and (optional) language, followed by a series of items, each of which has a title, link, and description.

The Channel. The channel is a required element that provides information about your RSS feed, including the channel name, who created it, its description, its language, and a URL. In addition to the required title, link, and description elements, channels can have some optional tags. These include PICS rating, copyright identifier, publication date, and webmaster. Thus for the ACME podcast series, the channel would give a general description of the purpose of the ACME series.

Items. Items, which contain the channel content, are the most important elements in a channel. While the other elements in the channel are usually static, each time you update your podcast, you will also update the item.

Items require three elements: title, link, and description. In typical use, the RSS title is usually rendered as a headline, the description as a one- or two-paragraph teaser, and the URL as a hyperlink to the full article or file.

Each item provides information about one program. Thus, each new episode of the ACME 360 podcast would be an item. The feed would provide information about the latest topics covered in the training podcast.

See the box for an example of what the RSS feed for the ACME podcast might look like.

Sample RSS Feed Text

```
<?xml version="1.0"?>
<rss version="2.0">
<channel>
<title>ACME 360 Podcast</title>
<link>http://www.acmepodcast.com/</link>
<description>Updates to the ACME Business Tool
</description>
<language>en-us</language>
<copyright>Copyright 2007 ACME Podcast</ copyright>
<item>
<title>New Functionality</title>
<link>http://www.ACMEPodcast.com/ACME/ACME2.
html</link>
```

```
<description>New Inventory Control Feature Released.
</description>
<enclosure url="http://www.acmepodcast.com/updates/latest_
news.mp3" length="640561" type="audio/mpeg"/>
</item>
</channel>
</rss>
```

As mentioned earlier, the effort required to create this feed will vary, depending on whether the podcast will reside on an organization's internal intranet or on the Internet. If your organization is planning on hosting the podcast on its internal servers, having the podcast tool generate the RSS feed is probably not an option. If the podcast will be hosted on a service such as iTunes or mac then there is virtually no work required.

Here's what it would take to publish the ACME podcast.

Manually Creating RSS Feeds

As we indicated earlier, items are the heart of any RSS file. To manually create such a file, you could use any text editor to type in the code and then copy and paste the code into your Web page, or if you know how to use an HTML editor, you can enter the code there. All podcasts have at least one item or Web page that you'd like learners to link to. For example, let's say we've just created a new podcast in the ACME 360 series that discusses a new accounting feature. Information about that podcast file would form an item that we would need to enter into the RSS file.

To enter the item into the RSS file, we would need three bits of information:

- Title
- Description
- Link

The title and description of the item do not need to exactly match the HTML title tag of the file that the item refers to. Any title and description that describes the file will be sufficient. Using the file's title, however, makes it easy to copy and paste to build your RSS feed.

In this case, let's say we settle on the following information to define it as an item:

- *Title:* ACME Adds Accounting Functionality
- *Description:* End users, technical experts, and management show how to apply this new enhancement.
- *Link:* http://www.acmepodcast.com/updates/latest_news.mp3

To create the RSS file we would need to surround the title, description, and link information with XML tags. XML tags are similar to HTML tags, except that XML tags have no set definitions. That is, anyone can make up a particular XML tag. Whether it is useful depends on the program that reads the resulting XML file. In the case of RSS feeds, they have their own unique set of defined XML tags. Use these correctly, and anything that reads RSS will understand your information.

Here's how you might create an XML tag for our sample podcast.

1. Enter a <title> tag, followed by the text of the title, then closed with another </title> tag. It would look like this:

   <Title> ACME Adds Accounting Functionality </title>

2. Enter a description. Begin with a <description> tag, and then follow with the actual description. Close with another </description> tag:

   <Description> End users, technical experts, and management show how to apply this new enhancement. </description>

3. Add the link information. Start with <link>, enter the actual hyperlink where the podcast will be found, then close with </link>:

```
<Link>
http://www.acmepodcast.com/updates/latest_news.mp3
</link>
```

4. Define all this information as forming a particular "item" by using a special item tag <item> at the beginning and the end of the information. The finished product would look like this:

```
<item>
<title> ACME Adds Accounting Functionality </title>
<description> End users, technical experts, and
management show how to apply this new enhancement.
</description>
<link>
http://www.acmepodcast.com/updates/latest_news.mp3
</link>
</item>
```

If you have other items you want to make available for subscription, you can simply add more item elements, following the same procedure. The common practice is for new items to be inserted at the top, with old items removed from the bottom, to make room for new items.

After creating or generating the RSS file, you need to test it—that is, to make sure it is valid before publishing it. Several validation services are available online. Just paste in the RSS feed's URL in the appropriate place on the service's Web site, submit, and the sites will validate that the RSS file works.

After the feed has been validated, it can be announced on a public area of the organization's site. Many podcasters use the XML logo to indicate that an RSS feed for the site is available.

Tools for Creating a RSS feed

While the process may seem complicated, creating an RSS file manually is as easy as taking an example file, like the one shown in the box earlier, opening it up, and entering the new information. In practice, however, most RSS files are generated automatically since almost all blogging programs and services have built-in features that generate RSS feeds.

These approaches include using an automatic RSS creator, having the blog build the feed, and using a stand-alone application.

Automatic RSS Creators. These days, you can find hundreds of Web sites and Java code snippets on the Internet that will automatically generate RSS based on the information contained on the MP3's ID3 tag. Simply make sure that all the information that you want to end up in the feed is included in the ID3 tag.

While this option is attractive and quick, it is also limiting if you need to include text links, images, and more information than is normally stored in an ID3 tag.

Blog Software. Any blog platform is able to take a post and add the appropriate RSS feed when a podcast is added. The blog post becomes the contents of the description tag, and the title of the post becomes the title tag. You will be prompted to designate the file to be attached as an enclosure that will be automatically built into the feed code. When the blog post is published it will create and post an update to the XML file.

Stand-Alone Applications. stand-alone applications can create beautiful and robust RSS without the need to use a blog to post the code. Applications such as Feeder (http://reinvented software.com/feeder/) work much in the way a blog platform does except that they don't publish blog posts. The only downside of this choice is that it causes duplicate work because you then need to update the Web site or blog and RSS separately.

Summary

Distribution is the final stage of the podcast development process. It is where the podcast is finally published to a Web page so that learners can access the content. The two major tasks that need to be accomplished during the distribution phase are to prepare the podcast for distribution, and then to upload the file to its final location.

This process can be very simple or moderately challenging, depending on the approach that you use. The approach will largely be affected by the organization's decision on where the podcasts will be located, the tools that have been used to produce the podcast, and whether the organization posts the podcast to a Web site or to a blog site. If the podcasts will be housed on internal servers and will be created with PC-based software, chances are that you will be required to write XML code to distribute the podcast. If the organization is open to a hosted Internet solution and can develop the podcasts on podcasting software, then distribution can be as simple as the click of a button.

Afterword

Podcasting is here to stay. Every day, additional podcasting products and services become available to users. The same excitement and growth that is taking place in the podcasting world in general is also taking place in the training podcasting space. At the time of this writing, the podcast directory (www.podcast.net) maintained a catalog of close to two thousand podcasts that were categorized as learning and instruction. A simple Google search on the phrase "training podcasts" brings back over sixty million hits.

The adoption and practical application of podcasting seems to be inevitable. As the technology becomes more commonplace in the larger environment, it seems natural that the training world will follow suit. Forrester Research (www.forrester.com), an independent technology and market research company, projected that in 2006 only 700,000 households in the United States would use podcasting. That number, however, would grow to 12.3 million households by 2010 (http://blogs.forrester.com/charleneli/2006/04/forrester_podca.html).

To give some context, the expectation of MP3 adoption was for about 11 million U.S. households in 2006, growing to 34.5 million households by 2010. This means in four years, about a third of the MP3 owners will be listening to podcasts on those devices. Podcasting will get easier and the content will get better.

As a formal, recognized medium of training distribution with a formal process for development, however, podcasting is in its infancy. The training field needs a formal methodology and approach specifically designed to support podcast development. Unlike traditional training programs, podcasts are in fact productions similar to movie, television, or recorded radio programs, and thus a development approach more in line with film production is the most appropriate. This book presents such an approach, introducing you to the concept, pre-production, production, post-production, and distribution stages and overlaying them with the DMADDI approach for developing instruction. I hope that armed with this book you are now ready to take the leap and create your own podcast. Good luck and good podcasting.

Appendix 1

WINDOWS PODCASTING SOFTWARE

BlogMatrix Sparks

An all-in-one podcasting solution that lets you record, mix, share, publish, store, and listen.

ePodcast Creator

An integrated podcasting application that lets you record, edit, create an RSS feed, and upload your podcast.

ePodcast Producer

All-in-one software package for podcasting that will record, edit, create an RSS feed, and upload your podcast, all from within one handy interface. In addition to the features of iPodcast Creator, Producer offers RealAudio compatibility, integrated CD ripping, and other features.

Escapepodder

Software that automatically generates an RSS feed and HTML for podcasts based on MP3s in a directory.

FeedForAll

An application that streamlines creating and publishing RSS feeds.

Folio First

Knowledgebase application with RSS and podcast support.

Free Podcast Maker

Simple tool for creating podcast XML files.

MixCast Live

Software that lets you record podcasts, create show notes, and publish feeds.

Podcast Accelerator

Podcast module for the NexGen Digital automation system.

Podcast AutoCue

Computer podcast cueing software; displays your text in a scrolling window.

Podifier

A simple-to-use application that automates the creation of an RSS feed, the enclosure of one or more MP3 files, and the use of a built-in ftp application to upload them to a server.

PodProducer

A free Windows podcasting application.

Propaganda

Software for recording, editing, and publishing podcasts.

RecorderPro

RecorderPro produces professional-quality podcast recordings in MP3 format. The VoiceBoost feature performs the same signal enhancement used on radio broadcasts for clarity and presence. The recording undo feature allows you to record in sections for perfect presentations.

Synclosure

Synclosure is a RSS aggregator to flexibly download files in enclosures. It supports filter keywords, custom actions, and a caching mechanism. (Source code available for other platforms.)

Webmaster Podcaster

Windows application for creating RSS/XML feeds for podcasts.

WebPod Studio

Software for creating audio and video podcasts. Comes in three editions: Standard, Professional, and Enterprise.

Winpodcast

Free application for creating podcasts.

Appendix 2

MACINTOSH PODCAST SOFTWARE

Cast Easy

An application designed to help users create, publish, and organize new and previously published podcasts.

Feeder

An application for creating, editing, and publishing RSS feeds.

FeedForAll

An application that streamlines creating and publishing RSS feeds.

Free Podcast Maker

Simple tool for creating podcast XML files.

Podcaster

Application to create podcasts and enhanced podcasts.

Podifier

A simple-to-use application that automates the creation of an RSS feed, the enclosure of one or more MP3 files, and the use of a built-in ftp application to upload them to a server.

ProfCast

An all-in-one presentation to podcast tool for the Mac. ProfCast provides tools for lecturers to create podcasts from their lectures, offering an integrated workflow for creating, recording, and publishing podcasts. ProfCast is a great choice for podcasts that are simple lectures—and also for presentations that include more complicated interactions. ProfCast is also an excellent tool when the participants of the podcast live in different geographic locations. Another benefit of ProfCast is that it has virtually no learning curve. The power of Keynote or PowerPoint and all the graphic and animation capability can be used with ProfCast. All elements of a presentation, including slide timing and voice narration, are captured with ProfCast and then published to the Web as a podcast, complete with RSS support.

RapidWeaver

Easy-to-use blogging tool that supports podcasting.

Appendix 3

AUDIO RECORDING SOFTWARE

While it might be expedient for small training organizations with limited resources to use podcasting applications (so that all development is done in one place with one tool), organizations with more resources or more talented developers might consider using multiple tools for podcast development (beginning with a robust audio recording tool). The benefit that you get from using this approach is the higher quality of the applications that were developed for a single purpose. Applications designed to record, edit, mix, and publish simply cannot compete with applications designed to just record.

The audio recording software that you choose will have as much of an influence on your podcasting experience as the hardware that you use. The major differences between any of the audio recording packages listed in this section are how many features are built into each and how well the packages may or may not handle production and post-production activities. Regardless of which audio recording package your organization chooses, however, the quality of the podcast will depend most on the sound going into the computer.

Apple GarageBand

Some of the most successful podcasts are produced using Garage-Band. The application is included in the iLife suite on all new Apple Macintosh computers. GarageBand has an easy-to-use and easy-to-understand interface and is more than capable enough for all but the most demanding podcasters. I believe GarageBand is the best application available for podcasting. Its only drawback is that it is available only to users of Macintosh computers.

Audacity

Audacity is a free and open-source software package for recording and editing sound. Audacity is also a multi-track application. This means that you can record one track, stop, and then record another track over the first. The benefit of multi-track applications is that they allow the users to add music and sound effects to a recording after the initial take. Audacity is available for virtually all computers—Macs, PCs, and machines running Linux.

Audio Hijack Pro

Audio Hijack Pro is a recording application for Mac OS X. It can record audio from one application or from all applications running. This feature makes it an invaluable tool for Mac users, especially those who want to record their voice, music, and live callers all at the same time.

BIAS Peak

BIAS Peak is an industry-standard stereo audio recording, editing, and processing application also for the Mac OS. It is the ideal audio utility for podcasters, audio professionals, and enthusiasts. In addition to fast and powerful audio editing, Peak integrates a wide variety of effects and signal processing tools to create custom fades, adjust audio gain, repair digital audio spikes, add real room ambience, change pitch and duration independently, and more, all while offering additional real-time effects such as parametric equalization, compression and limiting, reverb, dozens of other special effects, and access to third-party VST and Audio Unit plug-ins, or additional solutions from BIAS, such as the highly acclaimed SoundSoap family of audio noise reduction and restoration tools.

CastBlaster

CastBlaster was developed for podcast production and gives the user availability to play audio files while recording. Songs, promos, phone messages, and more can be preloaded into memory. During the recording session, these sounds can be played and recorded along with the podcaster's voice. CastBlaster acts essentially like a software version of an external mixer; each audio "input" has its own level controls and is mixed with the mic inputs and recorded along with them.

DSP–Quattro

DSP-Quattro is a professional creative tool for audio editing, plug-in hosting, and CD mastering. It includes a variety of recording and editing features to ensure that output is recorded just as you hear it and edited to perfection using editing functions and digital effects.

Sony Sound Forge

Sony Sound Forge, formerly known as Sonic Foundry Sound Forge, is a digital audio editing and creation suite aimed at the professional as well as the semi-professional market.

Appendix 4

A PODCASTER'S GLOSSARY

Advanced Audio Coding

Advanced Audio Coding (AAC) is a standardized digital audio compression scheme. It was developed with the cooperation and contributions of a group of companies, mainly Dolby, Fraunhofer (FhG), AT&T, Sony, and Nokia, and was officially declared an international standard by the Moving Pictures Experts Group in April 1997. It was written into specification as Part 7 of the MPEG-2 standard, and again into Part 3 of the MPEG-4 standard. As such, AAC can be referred to as MPEG-2 Part 7 and MPEG-4 Part 3, depending on its implementation, but is most often referred to as MPEG-4 AAC, or AAC for short. However, "MP4" usually refers to the format described in MPEG-4 Part 14, which is a container format for carriage of video and audio data.

AAC was promoted as the successor to MP3 for audio coding at medium to high bitrates. Its popularity is currently maintained by its status as the default iTunes codec—the media player that powers iPod, the most popular digital audio player on the market.

Aggregator

An *aggregator* (sometimes called a feed reader) is client software that uses a Web feed to retrieve syndicated content such as weblogs, podcasts, vlogs, and mainstream mass media Web sites, or in the case of a search aggregator, a customized set of search results.

Aggregators reduce the time and effort needed to regularly check Web sites for updates, creating a unique information space or "personal newspaper." Once subscribed to a feed, an aggregator is able to check for new content at user-determined intervals and retrieve the update. The content is sometimes described as being "pulled" to the subscriber, as opposed to "pushed" with e-mail or IM. Unlike recipients of some pushed information, the aggregator user can easily unsubscribe from a feed.

Aggregator features are being built into portal sites such as My Yahoo! and Google, modern Web browsers, e-mail programs like Mozilla Thunderbird, Apple's iTunes (which serves as a podcast aggregator), and other applications. Devices such as mobile phones and TiVo video recorders (already aggregating television programs) also incorporate XML aggregators.

The aggregator provides a consolidated view of the content in a single browser display or desktop application. Such applications are also referred to as RSS readers, feed readers, feed aggregators, news readers, or search aggregators.

The syndicated content an aggregator will retrieve and interpret is usually supplied in the form of RSS or other XML-formatted data, such as RDF/XML or Atom.

American Society of Composers, Authors, and Publishers

The *American Society of Composers, Authors, and Publishers* (ASCAP) is a performing rights organization, that is, it protects its members' musical copyrights, ensuring that when their copyrighted music is broadcast or otherwise publicly performed, whether live or recorded, it is properly licensed by the music users to compensate the creators of that music. In the United States, ASCAP competes with two other performing rights organizations: Broadcast Music Incorporated (or BMI) and SESAC.

ASCAP was established in New York City on February 13, 1914, to protect the copyrighted musical compositions of its members, then mostly the U.S. Tin Pan Alley music business. Both BMI and ASCAP, as well as other organizations like SESAC, monitor performances of the music of their respective members and collect and distribute royalties. ASCAP collected $749 million in licensing fees in 2005, and claims 235,000 song-writer, composer, and music publisher members.

Radio stations originally only broadcast performers live, with the performers working for free. Later, performers wanted to be paid and recordings became more palatable. Many composers didn't want their music performed or played for free, but the stations wouldn't pay them. The composers who were members of ASCAP boycotted radio in 1944. The stations established a competing source of music, Broadcast Music Incorporated (BMI). Many stations also joined one of the NBC networks, Red or Blue, to lower production costs. (The NBC Blue network later became ABC.)

Audio Interchange File Format

Audio Interchange File Format (AIFF) is an audio file format stan-dard used for storing sound data on personal computers. The for-mat was co-developed by Apple Computer based on Electronic Arts Interchange File Format (IFF) and is most commonly used on Apple Macintosh computer systems. AIFF is also used by Silicon Graphics Incorporated.

The audio data in an AIFF file are uncompressed big-endian pulse-code modulation (PCM), so the files tend to be much larger than files that use lossless compression (such as FLAC) or lossy compression formats such as Vorbis and MP3. Uncom-pressed AIFF files at compact-disc settings (44.1K samples/sec, 16 bits, 2 channels) thus have a bitrate of 1411.2 kbit/s. The AIFF-Compressed (AIFF-C or AIFC) format supports compres-sion ratios as high as 6:1.

An AIFF file is divided into a number of chunks. Each chunk is identified by a chunk ID known as an OSType.

Atom

Atom or *Atom Syndication Format* is an XML language used for Web feeds, while the *Atom Publishing Protocol* (APP for short) is a simple HTTP-based protocol for creating and updating Web resources.

Web feeds allow software to check for updates published on a Web site. To provide a Web feed, a site owner may use specialized software (such as a content management system) that publishes a list (or *feed*) of recent articles or content in a standardized, machine-readable format. The feed can then be downloaded by Web sites that syndicate content from the feed, or by feed reader programs that allow Internet users to subscribe to feeds and view their content.

A feed contains entries, which may be headlines, full-text articles, excerpts, summaries, or links to content on a Web site, along with various metadata.

The development of Atom was motivated by the existence of many incompatible versions of the RSS syndication format, all of which had shortcomings, and their poor interoperability.

Bitrate

Bitrate (sometimes written bit rate) is the number of bits that are conveyed or processed per unit of time. In digital multimedia, bitrate is the number of bits used per unit of time to represent a continuous medium such as audio or video. It is quantified using the bit per second (bit/s) unit or some derivative such as Mbit/s.

While often referred to as "speed," bitrate does not measure distance/time but quantity/time, and thus should be distinguished from the "propagation speed" (which depends on the transmission medium and has the usual physical meaning).

Broadcast Music Incorporated

Broadcast Music Incorporated (BMI) is a performing rights organization. It collects license fees on behalf of its members, who are songwriters, composers, and music publishers, and distributes the fees as royalties to those members whose works have been performed.

BMI was founded by radio executives in 1939 to provide competition in the field of performing rights, to assure royalty payments to writers and publishers of music not represented by the existing performing rights organizations, and to provide an alternative source of licensing for all music users.

Clipping

Clipping occurs when the signal is restricted by the range of a chosen representation. For example, in a system using 16-bit signed integers, 32,767 is the largest positive value that can be represented, and if during processing the amplitude of the signal is doubled, sample values of 32,000 should become 64,000, but instead they are truncated to the maximum, 32,767. Clipping is preferable to *wrapping*—the alternative in digital systems—which occurs if the digital hardware is allowed to overflow, ignoring the most significant bits of the magnitude, and sometimes even the sign of the sample value, resulting in terrible modification of the signal.

Codec

A *codec* is a device or program capable of performing encoding and decoding on a digital data stream or signal. The word codec may be a combination of any of the following: *Compressor-Decompressor*, *Coder-Decoder*, or *Compression/Decompression algorithm*.

Codecs encode a stream or signal for transmission, storage, or encryption and decode it for viewing or editing. Codecs are often used in videoconferencing and streaming media solutions. A videocamera's ADC converts its analog signals into digital signals, which are then passed through a video compressor for digital transmission or storage. A receiving device then runs the signal through a video decompressor, then a DAC for analog display. A codec is a generic name for a video conferencing unit.

An audio compressor converts analog audio signals into digital signals for transmission or storage. A receiving device then converts the digital signals back to analog, using an audio decompressor, for playback.

The raw encoded form of audio and video data is often called *essence,* to distinguish it from the metadata information that together make up the information content of the stream and any *wrapper* data that is then added to aid access to or improve the robustness of the stream.

Cost per click

Cost per click (CPC), sometimes referred to as "pay per click," is an advertising technique used on Web sites, advertising networks, and search engines.

Advertisers bid on keywords that they believe their target market (people they think would be interested in their offer) would type in the search bar when looking for that type of product or service. For example, an advertiser who sells red widgets would bid on the keyword "red widgets," hoping a user would type those words in the search bar, see the ad, click on it, and buy. These ads are called "sponsored links" or "sponsored ads" and appear next to and sometimes above the natural or organic results on the page. The advertiser pays only when the user clicks on the ad.

Cost per thousand

Cost per thousand or cost per mille (abbreviated as CPT or, more commonly, CPM) is used in marketing as a benchmark to calculate the relative cost of an advertising campaign or an ad message in a given medium. Rather than an absolute cost, CPM estimates the cost per thousand views of the ad.

For example, while the Super Bowl has the highest per-spot ad cost in the United States, it also has the most television viewers annually. Consequently, its CPM may be comparable to a less expensive spot aired during standard programming.

Creative Commons

Creative Commons is a nonprofit organization devoted to expanding the range of creative work available for others legally to build upon and share. The organization has released several copyright licenses known as Creative Commons Licenses.

The Creative Commons enables copyright holders to grant some of their rights to the public while retaining others through a variety of licensing and contract schemes including dedication to the public domain or open content licensing terms. The intention is to avoid the problems current copyright laws create for the sharing of information.

The project provides several free licenses that copyright owners can use when releasing their works on the Web. They also provide RDF/XML metadata that describes the license and the work, making it easier to automatically process and locate licensed works. Creative Commons also provide a "Founders' Copyright" contract, intended to re-create the effects of the original U.S. Copyright created by the founders in the U.S. Constitution.

Decibel

Decibel (dB) is a measure of the ratio between two quantities, and is used in a wide variety of measurements in acoustics, physics, and electronics. While originally only used for power and intensity ratios, it has come to be used more generally in engineering. The decibel is widely used in measurements of the loudness of sound. It is a dimensionless unit like percent. Decibels are useful because they allow even very large or small ratios to be represented with a conveniently small number (similar to scientific notation).

Domain names

Domain names are hostnames that provide more memorable terms to stand in for numeric IP addresses. They allow for any service to move to a different location in the topology of the Internet (or an intranet), which would then have a different IP address. By making possible the use of unique alphabetical addresses instead of numeric ones, domain names allow Internet users to easily find and communicate with Web sites and other server-based services.

Digital signal processing

Digital signal processing (DSP) is the study of signals in a digital representation and the processing methods of these signals. DSP and analog signal processing are subfields of signal processing. DSP has at least three major subfields: audio signal processing, digital image processing, and speech processing.

Equalization

Equalization (EQ) is the process of changing the frequency envelope of a sound. When a signal passes through any channel, temporal and frequency spreading occurs. Etymologically, to *equalize* means to correct, or make equal, the frequency response of a signal. The term *equalizer* is often incorrectly applied as a general term for audio filters, but only when audio filters are arranged so as to reverse the effects of the internal circuitry on sound output are they operating as equalizers.

Federal Communications Commission

The *Federal Communications Commission* (FCC) is an independent U.S. government agency, created, directed, and empowered by Congress.

The FCC was established by the Communications Act of 1934 as the successor to the Federal Radio Commission, and it is charged with regulating all non–federal government use of the radio spectrum (including radio and television broadcasting), and all interstate telecommunications (wire, satellite, and cable) as well as all international communications that originate or terminate in the United States. It is an important factor in U.S. telecommunication policy. The FCC took over wire communication regulation from the Interstate Commerce Commission.

File transfer protocol

File transfer protocol (FTP) is a commonly used protocol for exchanging files over any network that supports the TCP/IP protocol (such as the Internet or an intranet). Two computers are involved in any FTP transfer: a server and a client. The FTP server, running FTP server software, listens on the network for connection requests from other computers. The client computer, running FTP client software, initiates a connection to the server. Once connected, the client can do a number of file manipulation operations: upload files to the server, download files from the server, rename or delete files on the server, and so on. Any software company or individual programmer is able to create FTP server or client software because the protocol is an open standard. Virtually every computer platform supports the FTP protocol.

HyperText Markup Language

HyperText Markup Language (HTML) is the predominant language for the creation of Web pages. It provides a means to describe the structure of text-based information in a document—by denoting certain text as headings, paragraphs, lists, and so on—and to supplement that text with interactive forms, embedded images, and other objects. HTML can also describe, to some degree, the appearance and semantics of a document, and can provide additional cues, such as embedded scripting language code, that can affect the behavior of Web browsers and other HTML processors.

ID3

ID3 is a metadata container most often used in conjunction with the MP3 audio file format. It allows information such as the title, artist, album, track number, or other information about the file to be stored in the file itself.

Internet service provider

An *Internet service provider* (ISP) is a business or organization that sells access to the Internet and related services to consumers. ISPs can be started by just about any individual or group with sufficient money and expertise. In addition to Internet access via various technologies such as dial-up and DSL, they may provide a combination of services including Internet transit, domain name registration, and hosting.

LAME

LAME is an open source MPEG-1 Audio Layer 3 (MP3) encoder. The name LAME is a recursive acronym for "LAME Ain't an MP3 Encoder," although the current version is, in fact, a stand-alone MP3 encoder.

Latency

Latency is a time delay between the moment something is initiated and the moment one of its effects begins. The word derives from the fact that during the period of latency the effects of an action are latent, meaning "potential" or "not yet observed."

Mastering

Mastering is the process of preparing and transferring recorded audio to a medium that will be used in the production of copies. The specific medium varies, depending on the intended release format of the final product. For digital audio releases, several master media are possible, and the choice is based on replication factory requirements or record label security concerns. The chosen medium is then used as the source from which all copies will be made.

MPEG-1 Audio Layer 3

MPEG-1 Audio Layer 3, more commonly referred to as MP3, is a popular digital audio encoding and lossy compression format, designed to greatly reduce the amount of data required to represent audio, yet still sound like a faithful reproduction of the original uncompressed audio to most listeners. It was invented by a team of European engineers who worked in the framework of the EUREKA 147 DAB digital radio research program, and it became an ISO/IEC standard in 1991.

PHP

PHP (PHP: Hypertext Preprocessor) is a reflective programming language originally designed for producing dynamic Web pages. PHP is used mainly in server-side application software, but can be used from a command line interface or in stand-alone graphical applications.

Podcast

A *podcast* is a multimedia file distributed over the Internet using syndication feeds, for playback on mobile devices and personal computers. The term, as originally coined by Ben Hammersley in an article in *The Guardian* February 12, 2004, was meant as a portmanteau of *broadcasting* and *iPod*. Like *radio*, it can mean both the content and the method of delivery; the latter may also be termed podcasting. The host or author of a podcast is often called a podcaster.

Pop filter

A *pop filter* or pop shield is an anti-pop noise protection filter for microphones. It serves to reduce popping and hissing sounds in recorded speech and singing.

A pop filter is normally composed of an acoustically semitransparent material such as nylon stretched over a circular frame, and often includes a clamp and a flexible mounting bracket. A cheap pop shield can be made from material from tights or stockings stretched over a piece of wire such as a bent coat hanger.

RSS

RSS (which stands for Really Simple Syndication, not that anyone uses anything but the acronym) is a simple XML-based system that allows users to subscribe to their favorite Web sites. Using RSS, webmasters can put their content into a standardized format, which can be viewed and organized through RSS-aware software or automatically conveyed as new content on another Web site.

Uniform Resource Identifier

A *Uniform Resource Identifier* (URI) is a compact string of characters used to identify or name a resource. The main purpose of this identification is to enable interaction with representations of the resource over a network, typically the World Wide Web, using specific protocols.

WAV

WAV (or WAVE), short for Waveform audio format, is a Microsoft and IBM audio file format standard for storing audio on PCs. It is a variant of the RIFF bitstream format method for storing data in "chunks," and thus also close to the IFF and the AIFF format used on Macintosh computers. Both WAVs and AIFFs are compatible with Windows and Macintosh operating systems. It takes into account some differences of the Intel CPU such as little-endian byte order. The RIFF format acts as a wrapper for various audio compression codecs. It is the main format used on Windows systems for raw audio.

Waveform

Waveform means the shape and form of a signal, such as a wave moving across the surface of water, or the vibration of a plucked string.

Windows Media Audio

Windows Media Audio (WMA) is a proprietary compressed audio file format developed by Microsoft. It was initially intended to be a competitor to the popular MP3 format, though in terms of popularity of WMA files versus MP3 files, this never came close to occurring. However, with the introduction of WMA Pro and Apple's iTunes Music Store, WMA has positioned itself as a competitor to the Advanced Audio Coding format used by Apple and is part of Microsoft's Windows Media framework.

XML

The *extensible markup language* (always referred to as XML) is a W3C-recommended general-purpose markup language for creating special-purpose markup systems, capable of describing many different kinds of data.

Appendix 5

TURNING PRESENTATIONS INTO PODCASTS

ProfCast is a tool that can quickly convert lectures—as well as presentations that include more complicated interactions—into podcasts. This approach is especially attractive if PowerPoint or Keynote was used as a storyboard.

ProfCast requires virtually no time to learn. The power of Keynote or PowerPoint and all the graphic and animation capability that those programs possess can be used immediately in ProfCast, because all elements of a presentation, including slide timing and voice narration, are captured and then published to the Web as a podcast, complete with RSS support.

In the case of the ACME podcast I've used as an example throughout this book, the participants can use PowerPoint to record their own portions of the presentation. The final product can then be assembled during post-production. ProfCast as a development tool also reduces the stress associated with scheduling resources since the participants all have the ability to record a PowerPoint presentation on their own time.

Once the PowerPoint has been saved, you simply launch the ProfCast application, which gives you a dialog box like the one in Figure A5.1.

The PowerPoint file is simply dragged onto the ProfCast application. Figure A5.2 shows what that looks like.

Clicking the "Start Recording" button will cause ProfCast to capture all the animations, transitions, and audio from the PowerPoint file. Clicking "Publish" then gives you the option to publish to the location of choice.

Figure A5.1 ProfCast Application

Figure A5.2 ProfCast PowerPoint

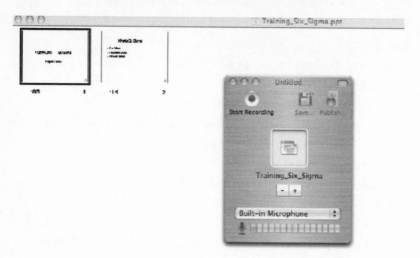

Appendix 6

HELPFUL PODCASTING RESOURCES

Academic MP3s–Is It iTime Yet?

www.campus-technology.com/article.asp?id=18001&p=1
A look at the use of podcasting in higher education; access date: February 23, 2007.

Beginners Guide to Podcast Creation

http://ipodlounge.com/index.php/articles/comments/beginners-guide-to-podcast-creation
A walk through the different elements you need to create a simple podcast, from computer and microphone through to the finished product; access date: February 23, 2007.

Exploiting the educational potential of podcasting

www.recap.ltd.uk/articles/podguide.html
Article written for teachers and senior leadership teams in schools. Provides a brief overview of podcasting and explores the potential of podcasting activities and scenarios for pupils and young people in schools. Access date: February 23, 2007.

How to Record a Podcast

www.macdevcenter.com/pub/a/mac/2005/01/25/podcast.html
For Macs, using Skype and other low-cost tools to go beyond GarageBand; access date: February 23, 2007.

iPod in Education

www.apple.com/education/solutions/ipod/

Case studies for using iPods in the classroom; access date: February 23, 2007.

The Pod People

www.elearningmag.com/ltimagazine/article/articleDetail.jsp?id= 301031

Article on the use of podcasting in corporate training; access date: February 23, 2007.

Podcast

From Wikipedia, the free encyclopedia:
http://en.wikipedia.org/wiki/Podcast

Concise definition and links to podcasting resources; access date: February 23, 2007.

Podcasting

http://engage.doit.wisc.edu/podcasting/

This site contains information on podcasting: what it is, and how to use it in teaching and learning; access date: February 23, 2007.

Podcasting for Education

www.darcynorman.net/2004/10/30/podcasting-for-education

Suggestions for using podcasts in education; access date: February 23, 2007.

Podcasting in Education

http://edupodder.com/

Suggestions for using podcasts in education; access date: February 23, 2007.

Podcasting Legal Guide

http://mirrors.creativecommons.org/Podcasting_Legal_Guide.pdf

A general road map of some of the legal issues specific to podcasting.

Podcasting Tools

www.podcasting-tools.com/

A comprehensive podcasting resource detailing everything you need to know about podcasting; access date: February 23, 2007.

Podcasting Tutorial

www.feedforall.com/podcasting-tutorial.htm

A step-by-step tutorial that explains how to set up a podcast; access date: February 23, 2007.

Seven things you should know about podcasting

www.educause.edu/ir/library/pdf/EL17003.pdf

Provides concise information on emerging learning practices and technologies.

Trend: Podcasting in Academic and Corporate Learning

www.learningcircuits.org/2005/jun2005/0506_trends

A basic explanation of podcasting, highlighting some of its uses in learning; access date: February 23, 2007.

When iPod goes collegiate

www.csmonitor.com/2005/0419/p11s01-legn.html

A review of the iPod pilot at Duke University; access date: February 23, 2007.

Index

ABOUT THE AUTHOR

Kaliym Islam has been nominated by TrainingIndustry.com as one of the "Top 20 Most Influential Training Professionals." He is a Six Sigma Black Belt, founder of Tek-Training LLC, and vice president of customer training and information products for the Depository Trust and Clearing Corporation (DTCC). At DTCC, he is responsible for the development and delivery of all customer-facing learning products. He is the author of *Developing and Measuring Training the Six Sigma Way* (Pfeiffer, 2006) in addition to this book, and he has been named a "Thought Leader" by TrainingOutsourcing.com's "Who's Who" selection committee. He is a pioneer in the application of Six Sigma methodologies to e-learning and an expert in facilitating change through redesign of internal operating and business processes.

Pfeiffer Publications Guide

This guide is designed to familiarize you with the various types of Pfeiffer publications. The formats section describes the various types of products that we publish; the methodologies section describes the many different ways that content might be provided within a product. We also provide a list of the topic areas in which we publish.

FORMATS

In addition to its extensive book-publishing program, Pfeiffer offers content in an array of formats, from fieldbooks for the practitioner to complete, ready-to-use training packages that support group learning.

FIELDBOOK Designed to provide information and guidance to practitioners in the midst of action. Most fieldbooks are companions to another, sometimes earlier, work, from which its ideas are derived; the fieldbook makes practical what was theoretical in the original text. Fieldbooks can certainly be read from cover to cover. More likely, though, you'll find yourself bouncing around following a particular theme, or dipping in as the mood, and the situation, dictate.

HANDBOOK A contributed volume of work on a single topic, comprising an eclectic mix of ideas, case studies, and best practices sourced by practitioners and experts in the field.

An editor or team of editors usually is appointed to seek out contributors and to evaluate content for relevance to the topic. Think of a handbook not as a ready-to-eat meal, but as a cookbook of ingredients that enables you to create the most fitting experience for the occasion.

RESOURCE Materials designed to support group learning. They come in many forms: a complete, ready-to-use exercise (such as a game); a comprehensive resource on one topic (such as conflict management) containing a variety of methods and approaches; or a collection of like-minded activities (such as icebreakers) on multiple subjects and situations.

TRAINING PACKAGE An entire, ready-to-use learning program that focuses on a particular topic or skill. All packages comprise a guide for the facilitator/trainer and a workbook for the participants. Some packages are supported with additional media—such as video—or learning aids, instruments, or other devices to help participants understand concepts or practice and develop skills.

- *Facilitator/trainer's guide* Contains an introduction to the program, advice on how to organize and facilitate the learning event, and step-by-step instructor notes. The guide also contains copies of presentation materials—handouts, presentations, and overhead designs, for example—used in the program.

- *Participant's workbook* Contains exercises and reading materials that support the learning goal and serves as a valuable reference and support guide for participants in the weeks and months that follow the learning event. Typically, each participant will require his or her own workbook.

ELECTRONIC CD-ROMs and web-based products transform static Pfeiffer content into dynamic, interactive experiences. Designed to take advantage of the searchability, automation, and ease-of-use that technology provides, our e-products bring convenience and immediate accessibility to your workspace.

METHODOLOGIES

CASE STUDY A presentation, in narrative form, of an actual event that has occurred inside an organization. Case studies are not prescriptive, nor are they used to prove a point; they are designed to develop critical analysis and decision-making skills. A case study has a specific time frame, specifies a sequence of events, is narrative in structure, and contains a plot structure—an issue (what should be/have been done?). Use case studies when the goal is to enable participants to apply previously learned theories to the circumstances in the case, decide what is pertinent, identify the real issues, decide what should have been done, and develop a plan of action.

ENERGIZER A short activity that develops readiness for the next session or learning event. Energizers are most commonly used after a break or lunch to stimulate or refocus the group. Many involve some form of physical activity, so they are a useful way to counter post-lunch lethargy. Other uses include transitioning from one topic to another, where "mental" distancing is important.

EXPERIENTIAL LEARNING ACTIVITY (ELA) A facilitator-led intervention that moves participants through the learning cycle from experience to application (also known as a Structured Experience). ELAs are carefully thought-out designs in which there is a definite learning purpose and intended outcome. Each step—everything that participants do during the activity—facilitates the accomplishment of the stated goal. Each ELA includes complete instructions for facilitating the intervention and a clear statement of goals, suggested group size and timing, materials required, an explanation of the process, and, where appropriate, possible variations to the activity. (For more detail on Experiential Learning Activities, see the Introduction to the *Reference Guide to Handbooks and Annuals*, 1999 edition, Pfeiffer, San Francisco.)

GAME A group activity that has the purpose of fostering team spirit and togetherness in addition to the achievement of a pre-stated goal. Usually contrived—undertaking a desert expedition, for example—this type of learning method offers an engaging means for participants to demonstrate and practice business and interpersonal skills. Games are effective for team building and personal development mainly because the goal is subordinate to the process—the means through which participants reach decisions, collaborate, communicate, and generate trust and understanding. Games often engage teams in "friendly" competition.

ICEBREAKER A (usually) short activity designed to help participants overcome initial anxiety in a training session and/or to acquaint the participants with one another. An icebreaker can be a fun activity or can be tied to specific topics or training goals. While a useful tool in itself, the icebreaker comes into its own in situations where tension or resistance exists within a group.

INSTRUMENT A device used to assess, appraise, evaluate, describe, classify, and summarize various aspects of human behavior. The term used to describe an instrument depends primarily on its format and purpose. These terms include survey, questionnaire, inventory, diagnostic, survey, and poll. Some uses of instruments include providing instrumental feedback to group members, studying here-and-now processes or functioning within a group, manipulating group composition, and evaluating outcomes of training and other interventions.

Instruments are popular in the training and HR field because, in general, more growth can occur if an individual is provided with a method for focusing specifically on his or her own behavior. Instruments also are used to obtain information that will serve as a basis for change and to assist in workforce planning efforts.

Paper-and-pencil tests still dominate the instrument landscape with a typical package comprising a facilitator's guide, which offers advice on administering the instrument and interpreting the collected data, and an initial set of instruments. Additional instruments are available separately. Pfeiffer, though, is investing heavily in e-instruments. Electronic instrumentation provides effortless distribution and, for larger groups particularly, offers advantages over paper-and-pencil tests in the time it takes to analyze data and provide feedback.

LECTURETTE A short talk that provides an explanation of a principle, model, or process that is pertinent to the participants' current learning needs. A lecturette is intended to establish a common language bond between the trainer and the participants by providing a mutual frame of reference. Use a lecturette as an introduction to a group activity or event, as an interjection during an event, or as a handout.

MODEL A graphic depiction of a system or process and the relationship among its elements. Models provide a frame of reference and something more tangible, and more easily remembered, than a verbal explanation. They also give participants something to "go on," enabling them to track their own progress as they experience the dynamics, processes, and relationships being depicted in the model.

ROLE PLAY A technique in which people assume a role in a situation/ scenario: a customer service rep in an angry-customer exchange, for example. The way in which the role is approached is then discussed and feedback is offered. The role play is often repeated using a different approach and/or incorporating changes made based on feedback received. In other words, role playing is a spontaneous interaction involving realistic behavior under artificial (and safe) conditions.

SIMULATION A methodology for understanding the interrelationships among components of a system or process. Simulations differ from games in that they test or use a model that depicts or mirrors some aspect of reality in form, if not necessarily in content. Learning occurs by studying the effects of change on one or more factors of the model. Simulations are commonly used to test hypotheses about what happens in a system—often referred to as "what if?" analysis—or to examine best-case/worst-case scenarios.

THEORY A presentation of an idea from a conjectural perspective. Theories are useful because they encourage us to examine behavior and phenomena through a different lens.

TOPICS

The twin goals of providing effective and practical solutions for workforce training and organization development and meeting the educational needs of training and human resource professionals shape Pfeiffer's publishing program. Core topics include the following:

Leadership & Management

Communication & Presentation

Coaching & Mentoring

Training & Development

E-Learning

Teams & Collaboration

OD & Strategic Planning

Human Resources

Consulting